JOURNEY IN

HIGHER
CONSCIOUS
AWAKENING

Dr. Marianne Maynard

STRATTON
—PRESS—
Publishing Life

JOURNEY IN HIGHER CONSCIOUS AWAKENING
Copyright © 2019 **Dr. Marianne Maynard**

Stratton Press Publishing
831 N Tatnall Street Suite M #188,
Wilmington, DE 19801
www.stratton-press.com
1-888-323-7009

ISBN (Paperback): 978-1-64345-313-2
ISBN (Ebook): 978-1-64345-473-3

Printed in the United States of America

This book is dedicated to all individuals,
who have agreed to use their inner spiritual guidance in
thoughts,words, and deeds, for the advancement of
higher conscious awakening on our beloved planet.

CONTENTS

INTRODUCTION

You are about to gain new insights about the evolutional cycles occurring on the planet and in human consciousness at this time. You will explore the planetary events occurring now and into the future, that will eventually change our views about life on Earth, higher heavenly planes, souls' ascension at death, and our afterlife journey. You will read about the role of angels in your life, and how you can communicate with Divine Spirit and deceased loved ones who reside on higher planes.

There is a steady flow of information about soul travel to higher planes, and after death experiences in books on the near-death experience, past life readings, and channeled messages from celestial beings. This book is based on a review of the literature, collective viewpoints from other authors, and my own personal experience, as cited in the text and reference pages.

Many are eagerly awaiting the great shift in human consciousness and earth changes foretold long ago. We want to know what to expect and how to prepare for this coming events in world history. As humans evolve to the next phase of our evolution, guidance will come from the celestial realms to lead the way. The intent of the book is to alert readers to the waves of the higher planetary frequencies that are transforming our planet and human consciousness. This new influx of cosmic energy will eventually enable humanity to advance spiritually, and experience more enlightenment, and peaceful, harmonious lives. You will want to share this book with your friends and review it often as you observe and experience planetary changes and the impact on your life now and into the future.

PREFACE

You are about to discover the meaning of the evolution cycle occurring on the planet and in human consciousness at this time. You will explore the ascension process that humanity will experience in the coming years that will expand our acceptance of our multidimensional nature, including transition at death and the soul's afterlife journey. You will read about the role of angels in your life, and communication with Divine Spirit and deceased loved ones who reside on higher planes.

There is now a steady flow of information about near-death experience, past life readings and channeled messages from celestial beings. In addition, there is a growing body of information from metaphysics, vibrational medicine, ecology, quantum physics, human potential, planetary changes, natural healing, and physic phenomena that is available for review.

Many are eagerly awaiting the great shift in human consciousness and earth changes foretold long ago. We want to know what to expect and how to prepare for this coming age of enlightenment. We are now able to articulate the events that have lead us to this great shift. As we humans evolve to the next phase of our evolution, we will have access to information from the celestial realms. The intent of the book is to alert readers to the waves of the higher planetary frequencies that are transforming our planet and human consciousness. This influx of energy will eventually enable humanity to experience more enlightened, and harmonious lives.

Share this book with family and friends. Review it often as you observe and experience planetary changes and the impact on your life now and into the future. For I dedicate this book to all the fearless people who are participating in a renewal cycle of spiritual transformation and consciousness awakening on earth.

1

PLANETARY ASCENSION

Mother Earth Ascending

Ready or not, Mother Earth is ascending along with human collective consciousness. Humanity is currently experiencing an expanded awareness and a spiritual awakening. Earth movement, climate changes, and severe storms, are, in part, due to human collective thought patterns moving on high frequency waves, across space and time. Our thoughts create and maintain the reality we perceive. The people of the world are slowly waking up from a deep sleep of forgetfulness. We are becoming conscious of our responsibility and stewardship of Mother Earth; as she expresses her discontent, and shifts her body to accommodate internal and external cleansing. Concerned environmental groups around the world are also expressing discontent with the slow pace of clean-ing-up the planet, in order release the build-up of physical toxins and poisons.

Groups of concerned citizens are no longer willing to accept the status quo that doing business as usual is the best approach, and are seriously questioning our governmental and corporate leaders on their decisions and intentions. We have acknowledged that there are better approaches that will serve the good of all peoples of the world. Our current reality is changing because humanity is feeling unsafe, and melancholy about its vulnerable world and searching for new peaceful solutions to the world's many problems. More people are acknowledging that our planet and humanity seems to be going through an evolutional shift, and hope this will lead to a higher conscious awakening.

Moreover, many feel that there are unseen forces at work in the universe that has re-energized our solar system. We do not know what our planet and humanity will eventually evolve to at this time, because we are still creating our future. However, many more people today are searching for a spiritual purpose in life, and feel the flow of higher energy frequencies surrounding them. Some seek out alternative therapists who use higher energy frequencies for healing and balancing human energy fields, while others are exploring the use of higher frequencies to rebalance the earth's energy fields.

We can choose to accept what is, or to believe there is more to embrace in life. We can envision scenarios for ourselves and the planet that are more spiritual, loving, and peaceful than our present world. We can make a difference in the world by focusing our thoughts and actions on harmony, unity, and abundance for all. Let us continue to focus on peace and world enlightenment, and align our intentions with the collective forces for peace. Now and well into the future will be critical times for humanity to manifest the higher consciousness of love and light frequencies to heal the planet.

Our collective thoughts can create a world full of hope and abundance; or the opposite effect of fear, lack, and suffering. Often referred to as the "Law of Causation" or "Karma", we reap what we sow in life. Therefore, let us sow positive and loving thoughts, and pursue deeds of loving kindness and benevolent service; for abundance flourishes in a grateful heart. According to Ernest Holmes, author of *The Science of Mind,* the chain of causation can be set in motion, individually or collectively, and produces its inevitable results, unless it is changed. Humanity has in the past, and can again, during this period in world history, choose a higher state of consciousness in resolving personal, national and international conflicts and global disputes.

Furthermore, keep in mind that the cosmology of the universe is an orderly, harmonious system created from the one Divine Mind. Everything that is manifesting in the world, the good and the evil, began in the thoughts of humans as collective thought images before appearing in physical reality. Humanity has made an initial shift in consciousness by focusing more on creating world peace and prosperity for all peoples of the world. Therefore, let us continue to wholeheartedly direct our efforts towards a healthy and bountiful planet, in which humanity and nature can thrive together.

Viewpoints on Planetary Shifts

At this moment in time, Mother Earth, as an abused and battered spirit, plea to humanity is to help her heal. She greatly needs our prayers, love, and protection. To begin with, we can hold in consciousness and visualize a more beautiful and grander planet. We also can assist in the cleansing and renewal of Earth by encouraging our local and state agencies, and organizations, to sponsor projects that would create clean, healthy living environments for all people to enjoy. Our planet is a living breathing spirit and' from time to time, expresses her distress about our disregard for her gifts of bounty, natural beauty, and resources. Our planet is now speaking out, using the voice of storms, climate alter-nations, fires, earthquakes, and other calamities. We are told to expect more of the same as she shifts her magnetic energy field and moves into a new cycle of evolution. She is now re-balancing and cleansing her physical form and renewing her spirit, as we would do when our bodies are sick or injured.

We can expect that earth's realignment will take some time and result in more climate changes, such as, warming and cooling of the planet, melting of the polar ice caps, severe storms, flooding, drought, fires, increased volcanic activities, as well as land mass movements on the planet's surface and oceans' floor.

During critical planetary evolutionary changes the presence of celestial beings are more keenly felt, and noticeably expressed in nations' creative forms of art, dance, and music. All change, both planetary and societal, foster spiritual growth. Spiritual guides, and advanced souls have informed us that Earth changes will coincide with a spiritual renaissance on the planet, and a higher conscious reawakening. This will be an important period in the cycles of world's history - a new beginning for all life forms on the planet. Some of us are aware of, or, experiencing these changes now on an emotional, and physical level; and are so guided by our higher consciousness and intuitive minds to begin adapting to a more peaceful, healthy and spiritual form of living.

We find that the Hopi Indians and other Earth's indigenous peoples have also foretold this period in human history that is presently unfolding. "According to the ancient Mayans, the age we have been living in began August 13, 3113, BC, called the 'Age of Movement,' will end on December 22, 2013. The Navajo spoke of an age following this period, called the 'Age of Spirit of All Living Things,' will be a short age. Then to be followed by an age called 'Return to Oneness' (John Van Auken, *Birth Pains to a Golden Age*, A.R.E. Letter, May 8, 2006).

The potential to change the planet's future from that of total destruction to a consciousness of peace, love and joy has always been our choice. However, a critical mass of enlightened individuals with a focused intention on world peace was needed. This occurred during the Harmonic Convergence, August 17th –19th, 1987, when global prayers and celebration songs, on saving the planet, spread around the world. This global celebration of intention and commitment marked the beginning of a new evolutional cycle on the planet in tune with the cosmic universe cycles. Consequently, a new reality for world peace was reaffirmed during the observance of the Harmonic Concordance on November 8, 2003, when millions of people worldwide gathered for prayers for a more harmonious world. On this date, many witnessed a total lunar eclipse that coincided with the appearance of a Grand Sextile pattern, comprised of six planets; the Sun, Moon, Mars, Jupiter, Saturn, and Chiron, in the formation of a six-pointed star of David/Seal of Solomon pattern. Some saw this as a sign from heaven that meant positive results would come.

Since the Harmonic Convergence, Gregg Braden and other scientists have observed a measurable increase in the energy field on the planet. The earth's resonant frequency has increased to a fundamental vibration of 13 cycles per second (hertz), from the usual 8 Hz per second that was the norm for thousands of years. Accompanying this energy boost is a rapid decrease in the magnetic field that surrounds our planet. Braden predicts that the planet's magnetic field will eventually reach the zero point, along with an increased frequency rate. This change was collectively known by ancient peoples of the world as "the Shift of the Ages" (Gregg Braden, *Awakening to Zero Point,* 1997). Others have also reported measurable increase in the earth's energy field, a weakening of the magnetic field surrounding earth, and a shift in the earth's rotation and tilt. In addition to the above changes, there also appears to be a shift in human values, beliefs, and behaviors at this time.

Further evident of planetary changes is Lee Carroll's series of Kryon books that describes events leading up to the shift in Earth's magnetic grid, which settled in its' present pattern in 2003. Scientists also reported on the following events, believed to be related to planetary changes.

- *Meteorological:* increased activity of asteroids/comets near Earth.
- *Geological:* increase in the earth's resonance, (hertz) vibration units, causing more weather changes, severe storms, volcanic activity and earthquakes.
- *Spiritual:* increased energy and gamma ray activity, sunspots, flares and other cosmic activities affecting our biology, will enable us to accommodate higher energy frequencies and expand our awareness and spiritual consciousness.

Further, we find that James Tyberonn, a retired geologist, channels Archangel Matatron, authored articles in the *Journal of Emergence,* as well as books on planetary changes, has a different perspective on global warming. He views the primary causes, not so much as greenhouse gases and burning fossil fuels, but the spin velocity of the planet's inner core. He also suggests that "the changing torque and the increased pulses, that flow outward, contribute to the melting of the icecaps and the changing of air and water currents (Journal of Emergence, October, 2007). He views Earth changes as a necessary part of transition that will move the planet beyond the third dimension and into the fourth and higher dimensions. Consequently, he and others with similar viewpoints, feel that there is little we can do to prevent global warming, melting of icecaps, and rising sea waters that will inundate coastal land and small islands.

In addition, climatologists tell us that climate changes will bring on severe storms and flooding in some regions and hot, dry weather in other regions, along with the extinction of many plants and animal species. Most scientists agree that these planetary events are expected to continue and affect life on earth for some time. After all, it would seem for now that the suspected cause of planetary change is its hot liquid inner core, which influences the warming and cooling cycles of oceans' temperatures and weather patterns.

Another point-of-view is that the warming of the planet is contributing to the rising vibrational rate of the planet and its inhabitants, and the beginning step in a new evolutionary cycle. All life is vibratory and the higher a thing vibrates the less dense it becomes, as occurs in solids, liquids, air, and in electromagnetic observations. For example, all thought is energy vibrating at a higher frequency than matter. Physical matter is energy vibrating at a select range of frequencies, some so high that our physical senses cannot detect its presence.

Evolutionary Cycles

Past planetary cycles have resulted in economic, environmental, and social-political-cultural changes on the planet. The current climate cycle is even now affecting humans, plant, and animal life, the food and water supplies, and the oceans temperature, and levels. It is difficult to predict how these disruptions will impact our lives and when our weather patterns will stabilize. At this point, we can only hope that humanity will have the knowledge and capability to successfully adapt during these changing times.

Based on recorded historical and geological findings our planet has experienced many cycles of both major and minor climate changes, including warming and severe cooling periods, along with a reconfiguration of landmass and raising oceans. Earth has gone through minor and major cyclical changes that eliminated many former species on the planet and caused the adaptation and evolution of others. Some cycles lasted approximately four hundred years and up to two thousand year or more. Other cycles can last for one million years. During these change periods there were major reversals in the direction of the climate on Earth. According to the Mayan calendar, the year 2012 will bring an end to our planetary history, as we know it, and the beginning of a new 5,125-year cycle of peace on the planet.

Nevertheless, it is believed that all levels of physical manifestation will experience some growth and development during planetary change cycles. On the other hand, other life forms may become extinct. Many agree that evolutionary cycles are a part of the natural laws decreed in the beginning of time by the Divine Mind for all creation, without which no manifestation can occur or exist on the planet. Consequently, all manifestation of life, experiences natural cycles of progression and regression, birth and death, during designated time periods with the intended purpose of always evolving to ever-higher states of physical and mental development.

If you believe that evolution, the fundamental law of nature, and, the universal force that drives us towards perfection, and becoming higher vibrational, or light beings; than you would agree that all life forms and species on earth can evolve with humans, to a higher stage on the evolutionary cycle. Therefore, let us affirm that all life forms have purpose and serve with gratitude in supporting the survival of other life forms on earth. All living entities and species have basic needs for survival, which are protection, appreciation, and loving compassionate care. All desire to live in harmony with one another. In order for humans to advance to a higher state of consciousness they must value and respect all life, including plants and animals that provide nutrition and food for our physical bodies. This next evolutionary stage is not in the future – it is evolving now on planet and in human consciousness. Therefore celebrate –for you have chosen to be on Earth during this stage of your evolvement and to experience these dynamic changes.

Earth's Hidden Dimensions

Our planet has many dimensions and levels of life forms, extending to seen and unseen surface and interior life on earth. Our perception of life on Earth is limited to what is perceived by our five senses. Most people are unaware that there are many levels of life forms around us. Those more psychically aware can see and even communicate through thought with these unseen beings. Ancient myths and fairy tales have spoken about the light beings around us, and native and indigenous art has depicted their likenesses. They are often referred to in our literature as nature beings and fairies, spirit guides, little ones, and light beings. They are generally invisible to the naked eye. However, some clairvoyant individuals and perceptive children report seeing them in nature around water, trees, plants rocks and mountains. Some children have imaginary playmates that include these delightful beings, and may also include ghosts, deceased spirits and visitors from other planes and planets. Respecting their presence and contributions to the planet will eventually enable us to joyfully interact with the unseen world around us. Our earth companions are evolving, with humans, to higher states of universal consciousness where communication between species, creatures and entities will be possible.

There are other realities surrounding the planet beyond human perceptional field. Inner earth has hidden dimensions of nature spirits and energetic forms, which are interrelated and integrated in their divine planetary purpose of supporting life on the planet. We are now expanding our conscious awareness and advancing our knowledge about the role of earth's sacred sites, such as, Machu Picchu, The Grand Canyon, Mount Shasta, Sedona, and other global sites around the world. All have purpose in enhancing the energy fields on earth and connecting with cosmic energy fields though earth's vortex and portals, and ley lines.

After all, our human body shares similarities with Mother Earth - the living, breathing entity that is our earth home. The similarities include the cycles of growth, decline, and the expressions of pain, stress, joy, love, and beauty. Earth's ley lines are akin to our circulatory system. The points of ley lines intersections are the nerve centers of the planet and remind us of the meridian lines and energy centers on the human body. Our bodies will respond to our loving thoughts and caring nature, as also will the spirit of planet earth. When we respect Earth and acknowledge the intelligence that resides therein we are able to communicate with its living and breathing essence. The earth speaks to us in many ways. If we but listen, we can hear the sounds of Earth breathing, stretching, settling, yawning, and even belching. Astronauts have recorded the humming and ringing sounds of earth as it rotates and spins in space. The beautiful images of our planet, taken by astronauts who traveled to the Moon and back, were awe inspiring, and have engendered in us profound love and respect for our earthly home.

Support Mother Earth

We are now reaching the point where critical masses of humans have the capacity to assist in the regeneration of our planet. As we do this for Mother Earth, we also do it for our own healing, for we are one with our Earth home. Even though it is preordained that the cycle of planetary changes are necessary and will occur on time in order to advance humankind, we may still have the opportunity to modify the more severe and destructive aspects of those changes predicted long ago. Through the power of creative thought and action, we can modify our wasteful habits, protect our natural resources and preserve plant and animal life.

To begin with, there is no need to pollute, deforest, disfigure, destroy, and, plunder planetary resources for greed and profit. There is more than enough for all to share and thrive. This is a difficult lesson for our collective human consciousness to accept, but accept we must if we are serious about saving the planet. We must change old habits and beliefs, that greed is acceptable, and wastefulness must be tolerated in a growing society. Old habits will no longer be sustainable. On higher planes of existence, all life and natural resources are sacred, nurtured, and honored. Nothing is destroyed for the benefit of another. It is time for this universal principle to be practiced on Earth. It is time for humans to accept their divine nature, which honors and respects all life, and that which lives in nature, for all is an expression of Divine Spirit in action, and contributes to Earth's bounty. Eventually, in order to evolve to higher levels of spirituality a pure vegetarian diet is all our bodies will need. This will enable us to adapt to the higher frequencies on the planet, and advance more quickly on the evolutionary ladder.

Next, we must prevent our cities from becoming dead zones of concrete jungles, with polluted air, unsafe drinking water, poor sanitation, crime, homelessness, high-density buildings, and unsafe dilapidated housing. We must find ways to help Mother Earth breathe again; replenish her lungs with fresh air, and to send forth new life and bounty by planting more trees in both urban and rural areas. This we can do now, together, to create a planet of prosperity and beauty, and in harmony with nature. Let us be worthy citizens of the planet and by accepting responsibility for the following initiatives:

1. Support an ecologically sustainable society and the elimination of human wastefulness by promoting and participating in recycling and conservation efforts nationwide.

2. Use biodegradable building materials, such as natural woven fibers, bamboo, clay tiles, and encourage the use recyclable resources in order to reduce the overuse of wood products that depletes our forests.

3. Support local organic family farms. Grow produce all year round in climate controlled green houses near cites, reducing the interstate transporting of produce.

4. Support state laws that promote the preservation of open land, planting of trees and local plants, and beautification and reforestation projects.

5. Honor our planet as a sacred home for all life forms, by respecting and protecting their habitats.

6. Promote and use energy-efficient equipment and appliances, and encourage state governments to mandate utility companies to use more alternative clean energy sources, such as wind, solar, biomass products and other energy sources yet to be discovered.

7. Support laws for clean air, water, and proper disposal of waste products/pollutants, and research on renewable, biodegradable, and clean energy.

8. Encourage builders to add rooftop gardens to high-rise apartments, and office complexes and provide open landscaped areas, shade trees and natural green areas, which can help to cool and purify city air.

9. Remember to contemplate daily on the beauty, sacredness, and bounty of Mother Earth, and all

that dwell within and on the surface, including the higher conscious awakening of humanity.

Take these steps, and more, to improve the quality of life in our cities, for we can no longer wait for our government to take action. We must do our part by speaking-out and letting our voices be heard by telling big corporations to change the way they do business, and by boycotting companies that pollute, destroy and waste our resources. We must change our habits and lifestyle. Many precious life forms have been extinguished because of our wastefulness and disregard for their important role in maintaining the planet's health; for as Earth recovers its health and abundance, so shall we. The choices and decisions you make today are crucial in setting the course of Earth's recovery.

After all, we are spiritually interconnected working partners with Earth; neither can survive without the other. With climate changes in full progress we can only prepare and adapt physically and emotionally to a new way of living. Your inner wisdom will guide you in the appropriate actions to take to survive as Mother Earth rebalances her energies. Let us all work together, in a harmonious alignment with Earth, preparing the way for a new day on the planet. Time is running out on the old order and ways of living. We can expect during this time socio-economic disruptions as the Old World passes away. Public opinions have already shifted in support for world sociopolitical and economic restructuring, with emphasis on humanitarian outreach, ecological protection of resources, and peaceful solutions to world conflicts. I hope you will be among the many that support and work toward these positive changes for the planet.

The message I received from a higher spiritual source is that the much needed change on the planet has now arrived. Expect it to be gradual at first and then become more rapid in the coming years. Many will be forced to leave their homes and seek new locations. There will be large migrations of people from one location to another seeking shelter and new food sources. Governments will be hard pressed to improve the situation, for climate conditions and severe storms will come too quickly to manage and resettle the many people or prevent destructive outcomes. Unfortunately, disruption in our global communication and warning system will also slow the flow of information and thereby delay response and recovery action. This will create much fear and despair in the population. So take heed and begin to prepare now, especially if you live in areas that are most likely to be affected by Earth changes.

Spirit Message

Heavenly Spirit sources also inform me that:

> *Planet Earth is receiving help from the hierarchy of Celestial Beings (spiritual guides, angels, ascended masters, The Holy Spirit, advanced and departed souls, and many unnamed beings. They are prepared to guide humanity, and aid in our survival, if we but ask for their help. You are asked to eliminate the clutter in your lives and consider relocating to higher ground. Listen*

to your inner voice when making decisions, and let go of old thought patterns that are holding you back. These are exciting transforming times on earth, for peoples will witness the beginning of a New World in unity of purpose. Therefore, fear not, all will be well in the end, for the higher spiritual frequencies flowing to the planet are from Divine Source of all that is. You access this energy source by going within, where the kingdom of heaven resides. It is available to all loving hearts to use for healing, harmony, and peace in the world. We ask you to listen to living God within you, and be a channel for Divine wisdom and love that is flowing forth on planet in waves of Light and Sound.

The time is at hand when the peoples of Earth will accept their divine nature and willingly use the higher frequencies on Earth for peaceful solutions and prosperity for all. Those in fear, with closed hearts and minds, will go about their daily activities, unaware of the shift in human consciousness and Earth's energies, until they eventually come to realize the world is different and full of light. We are now in the midst of an ascension cycle that is leading us on a vertical path to higher conscious awakening. Let your intuition guide your destiny, for the door to new possibilities beckons you to pass through without delay.

2

AWAKENING TO NEW REALITIES

Ascending to Higher Consciousness

We have reached a point in our earthly journey where humanity is at the threshold of ascension, which includes transcending or rising above and beyond the limitations of our limited thought patterns, beliefs, and ideas of who we are and our purpose for being on Earth. We are coming to the realization that our self-centered thoughts have limited our perceptions. We now need to focus on God-centered thoughts, and the full expression of our divinity and spirituality. We are also becoming aware of our physical, mental, and emotional nature; and that we are indeed spiritual beings temporarily occupying physical bodies in a material world. This transcendence in consciousness has opened channels for God's light, love, and acceptance of

His divine plan for humanity's next evolutionary cycle on Earth.

Through prayer, meditation, and direct communication with Divine Spirit and celestial beings, we will receive revelatory information to assist our progress on Earth. Begin an inner dialogue with the God within you, your higher self, and record the words that come to you. Open your heart to the loving words from celestial beings and give thanks for their guidance and blessings. Everyone has access to celestial beings when the heart is open and full of love. When we ask for their guidance, we receive their blessings, for the only separation between the material and spiritual world is our thoughts and beliefs. Our angelic companions are standing by to assist us. Their messages of love and peace bring joy to the heart. Acknowledge and joyfully accept your spiritual companions and interdimensional helpers and be open to their daily guidance. You do this by listening and following your intuition, which is your higher consciousness speaking through you. You also receive guidance in your daily mediations and nightly dreams. When you ask for guidance in prayer, silence your mind's chatter, find that peaceful place within, and expect to receive a response.

Expanding Consciousness

Be ever mindful of your conscious thoughts and their focus. Observe how your consciousness shifts during brief interludes, from present time to past remembrance, and projects into the future. Observe how you combine new information with past experiences and apply them to present situations. Reliance on applying past experiences to resolve present problems may keep you stuck in the past and hinder living in the present, seeing possibilities, and awakening to a higher calling in life. Listen to what your current feelings, emotions and intuitions are telling you to do. It may be telling you to change your life in some way, pursue a new focus in life, or open your heart and mind to higher wisdom. If this is so, then pay attention and re-examine your present reality and surroundings and fearlessly take the action that is needed to move in a new direction.

These changing times require a change in focus, an alert mind, and the ability to understand what is occurring in your environment. The ability to be present, in the here and now, will enable you to face the cycles of change and replace fear with joyful anticipation. Living in the now will enable your heart and mind to receive guidance from your higher self—that divine source within that is constantly trying to get your attention.

Even now, some individuals are experiencing precognitive awareness of future events, those events that have not yet occurred in the present reality or visible to our physical senses. There are others who are *clairvoyance*, and are able to perceive objects and matter beyond normal sensory perception; and still more individuals who are *clairaudience*, and hear with their inner ear that which are not audible, or sound not present in to the outer ear in objective reality. Some are even having out-of-body soul travel experiences, projecting their consciousness to other dimensions and realities in the universe during periods of wakefulness and sleep. Evidently, these experiences will become normal occurrence for most people.

Our dreams are another source of information to higher conscious awakening. The unconscious self is free to speak to us in the symbolic language of dreams. As we dream, scenes, situations, images of deceased persons, and other dimensions are projected into our sleeping minds. We take the role of active participants in the dream scenario or the role of passive observers of events. Our roles may be restrained or free, with dream images, people, and locations rapidly changing with each new thought. Dreams can show the future, give clear messages and guidance, and alert us to conditions of which we are unaware in the waking world.

We often receive nightly instructions during sleep and find ourselves in classrooms, or being guided to the Hall of Learning in the higher heavenly realms. As you ascend in consciousness, expect to have vivid dreams that can be as real to you as your physical waking life – dreams in which you will perceive and communicate with your multidimensional self. In fact, many have reported insightful dreams concerning personal relationships, health issues, future events, and visits with deceased family members. Consider your dreams as steps on the path to your spiritual awakening. Sri Harold Klemp, The Mahanta, the Living ECK Master, reminds us that when we dream we leave our body and go to the dream world in full consciousness, which is the other real world in which we live beyond the physical plane. On many occasions we travel to the Astral Plane and assume an Astral body form to experience life on this plane, or travel further to the Causal, Mental, Etheric and higher spiritual planes where our self/soul realization expands to God consciousness.

It is important to record your dreams and learn to interpret the symbolic language of the soul, another source of information from your higher consciousness. Dreams have been used since early times as a source for guidance, insight, and as the door to other dimensions. I have found Ann Ree Colton's book, *Watch Your Dreams,* an important resource for understanding dream symbols. Colton has found that the veil between dreaming and waking consciousness is extremely thin in all persons having receptive and suggestible natures. If you are interested in learning more about out-of-body travel to other dimensions during sleep read Robert Monroe's, book, *Journeys Out of the Body.* He describes his many out-of-body trips to other realms and encounters with people from other dimensions while in a sleep-like state. Also Sri Harold Klemp's, *Soul Travelers of the Far Country* will provide valuable insights about this subject.

Jane Roberts, in *Seth Speaks,* informs us that "in our sleep and dream states, we are involved in the same dimension of existence in which we have our after-death experiences" (1972, 152). She adds, "the best way to become acquainted with the after-death reality ahead of time is to explore and understand the nature of our dreaming self" (p.154). I, too, encourage you to take your dreams seriously and write down the messages and events you recall when you awake while the dream is still fresh in your mind. In my book, *Take Charge of Your Thoughts - Create Your Ideal Life*, 2009, is a short form to request, record, and obtain information from your dreams. The unconscious mind sees and retains all that may not be

JOURNEY IN HIGHER CONSCIOUS AWAKENING

available to the conscious mind. Don't overlook this valuable source of guidance in your life.

At the Threshold of Ascension

Lee Carroll channels Kryon, who is an angel of magnetic service, guardian of earth, and is associated with Archangel Michael. Kryon has spoken many times about the coming period of human ascension. Ascension is often referred to as increasing the vibratory rate of our physical and higher energetic bodies while remaining on Earth. When we are experiencing a higher vibration, we become more God-centered, similar to the ascended masters. An ascended person takes on higher dimensional energies, accepts spiritual guidance, and expresses a higher purpose in life. We are told that our ascended status will be gradually reflected in our biology, our DNA, and our spiritual perceptions and inner knowing of our interdimensional nature. Prophecies suggest that our planet and the human race are on the verge of taking the next step in the evolutionary process of humankind. Are you ready to participate, bear witness, or serve as light workers in the ascension process on Earth?

You chose to be here on earth at this moment in time to celebrate God's divine plan for humankind, and to help create peaceful solutions to world problems. Science and technology are now at the threshold of new discoveries that will improve our quality of life. New information about human DNA will enable humans to extend their lives many more years. Also, in the coming years, our physicists and astronomers may possibly discover unlimited sources of energy in our galaxy. Eventually, there will be scientific confirmation that we are divine beings and coworkers in an unlimited, ever-expanding universe. Soon, it will be validated that our collective thoughts and the energy/light waves of love are the driving forces in the universe. Consider joining like-minded people in the world who are promoting harmony, integrity in the affairs of government and the corporate world, and above all, fairness and respect for all people worldwide.

As the consciousness of love on the planet increases, we will see a renaissance in music, creative arts, literature, and in the expression of higher spiritual aspirations and values. When the generation of Indigo, Crystal children, or children of light comes of age and assumes leadership positions in their respective countries, their views will be much different from today's leaders. These children and young adults are said to have the wisdom, intelligence, and openness to move societies forward in many areas. We can expect to see major changes in our educational, medical and social systems, in the way business and political affairs are conducted, and above all, a unifying spirit of brotherly/sisterly love, harmony and peace in the world. This new generation will be our future trailblazers.

The Kryon books describe these children as having higher vibrational frequencies, and thus the ability to avoid certain astrological attributes that have influenced us in the past. Their stronger biological makeup protects them from many environmental impurities and diseases that have plagued humans in the past. It is the hope of the world that when these special children become our future teachers, scientists, writers, artists, government workers, and political leaders, they will bring about a more loving, peaceful and compassionate society. Therefore, let us support this generation by being open to their intentions and join with them for a more progressive world.

When we reclaim our divinity, help will come from higher-dimensional guides to assist us. The veil between the dimensions is less dense now, providing opportunities to receive information and expand our spiritual nature and understanding. Do not be fearful to attune your thoughts to higher sources of wisdom and opening your hearts to the guidance and inspiration of the Divine Spirit, angels and other celestial beings. Be prepared to receive this in the form of dreams and intuition as well as telepathic messages. Our heavenly guides use these methods to communicate with us. Ask for guidance, listen for a response, and write down the message, which is always loving, healing, and reassuring.

As the Earth goes through its rebirth and cleansing process, there will be many disruptions in our normal living patterns. Begin now to identify what you would like to see manifested in your life, and join others on the path of self-realization, harmony, and world peace. Listen for inner guidance to find the best direction for you to pursue during these challenging times. When you ask for inner guidance, you will receive clear information regarding the best timing for action. Do not, out of fear, follow the herd instinct, which can lead you astray. Your inner wisdom and your guardian angels will show you the way to safety. Know that Spirit desires only good for you, and by asking for help from the highest source, it shall be given. Be not afraid of the changes that occur around you, be at peace, and know the purpose is divine order for our planet and its inhabitants. Release that which holds you back, such as material attachments, and trust with joyful anticipation the new opportunities waiting for your continued growth and enlightenment.

There are many articles and books about earth and climate changes, including potential scenarios for our future. We could have continuous wars or a life of peace, harmony and abundance. The question is – does humanity have the will, faith, and determination to choose wisely? We do know that before positive changes can occur, world societies will have to go through a disruption and dismantling of old ways, including a breaking up of old thought patterns, ways of conducting business, hatreds, fears, and divisions between people, after which reconstruction of a new world society can begin. This will be difficult and upsetting for many to adjust to while accepting a new way of living. If we wish to survive, humanity, as a whole must let go of old beliefs and ways of conducting business that divided people and disrespected their roles in society.

Consider what it would be like when the Earth's energy field shifts and there is a decrease in its gravitational pull. Perhaps you would feel physically and emotionally lighter. You may see yourself moving into a fifth-dimension reality, with expanded awareness, mental clarity, and telepathic communication, inter-dimensional and inter-planetary communication. You might be able to recall your past lives and your clarity about your soul's purpose. You could surround yourself in the divine light, hear the sound/voice of God, and serve as a co-worker with Divine Spirit. This could be our future reality as Earth transforms itself and moves into a higher dimension.

Ten Practical Steps in Moving Forward

Each person on the planet has the capacity to adapt to a new life that supports planetary changes and higher vibratory frequencies for conscious living. Consider the following suggestions to begin the process of conscious living and planting the seed for a new reality on Earth.

1. ***Accept Life Challenges***

    Each moment, you can choose to fulfill your soul's purpose: reuniting with the Divine Spirit. Each life lesson brings new insight of your role in demonstrating the source of divine love on Earth. You are here to express and demonstrate love, harmony, and peace on the planet. Center your thoughts, visions, and intentions on what your heart truly desires. Act on your intentions to express your life purpose a step at a time. Trust that your path will be made clear and your vision for peace and harmony manifested. Be confident in yourself and have faith that you have chosen wisely. The confirmation of your life purpose will be the joy and satisfaction you experience in life.

2. ***Pay Attention to Wake-Up Calls***

    Life is full of surprises. Often, just as you grasp your life's direction, a shift of events leads you in another direction. Surprise interludes from our Creator are for our growth and progress, for life was not meant to be humdrum and routine. From time to time, we are sent some nudges to wake us up and express our full potential. Expect and appreciate these wake-up calls. They help us reexamine our purpose in life and go that extra step to serve humanity in some unique way. Your intuition is your higher self, calling you to fulfill your destiny for spiritual growth. Messages for action can occur in many forms, including a series of unexpected incidents, new people appearing in your life, repeated messages from different sources, recurring dreams, and urges to make contact with others, or go to an event you would normally not consider. Pay attention, especially to those that persist or incidents that require full attention. Our environment also sends out signals to take action, move to a new location, and change our wasteful habits. These signs awaken our senses and awareness beyond our daily activities. We are also prone to shut out what we fear or do not wish to see, as well as shutting out people we don't understand or appreciate. We feel more protected staying in our cocoon, where a troubled world cannot harm us. Major calamities can be wake-up calls, moving humanity to notice those who need aid, compassion, and love. Responding to calls for help not only enhances our own spiritual growth but also unites us, as we reach out with love to all humanity.

3. *Let Go of the Past*

Holding on to old beliefs, habits, and things that clutter our lives keeps us from moving forward. Our desire for more, when we already have more than enough, limits the supply available for others. There is no need to keep what cannot be used or has lost its value; better to give items to those in need than to store them away unused. Forego greed and wastefulness and keep only that which is beneficial to your earthly journey, returning all else to the universal flow for redistribution. You can demonstrate the laws of supply and abundance by sharing and giving, which will release you from selfish attachments and the burdens they place on others. You leave all behind when departing from Earth, so travel lightly and appreciate the abundance that is yours now.

4. *Support Cooperation and Sharing*

Finding a community or study group that will support your spiritual and personal growth or organizations that promote peace and harmony in the world may be beneficial. Opportunities abound to serve humanity and use one's talents for good in the world. Whatever field your talents are in, such as art, science, education, healing, communication, business, technology, literature, agriculture or other areas, use your talents! Be generous in sharing your abilities with others. Teach what you know and lovingly give back the blessings you received

5. *Become Co-Workers*

The desire to create is a gift from Divine Spirit that seeks expression in the visible world. Great artists, composers, writers, inventors, and scientists visualized their creations prior to their manifestation on Earth. Let your inner vision show the path to your greatness and perfection as a divine work of art. Be true to yourself by freeing your creative spirit to be a partner in the co-creation process for a new day on Earth. Expand your consciousness and include all possibilities to bring the highest expression and good to humanity. Look for opportunities to work with others in healing the planet. Have patience and faith and know all is working in divine order

6. *Trust in Divine Order*

Peace of mind is your reward when you trust that divine order is operating in your life and your higher self has guided you to a higher purpose. Life is an adventure, so step aside and let your inner wisdom be your guide. Your past, present, and future is a living continuum in the here and now. Your higher consciousness prompts you to pursue certain life lessons and experiences in order to fulfill your spiritual purpose on Earth. Whatever your pursuits may be, plan to include humanitarian goals by promoting love, light, and peace on the planet.

7. *Let go of Fear*

Often fear holds us back from pursuing our goals. Fear not today or tomorrow, for all will be divinely cared for. Focus your attention on today's needs and release your fears of the unknown and unexpected. Replace your fears with feelings of gratitude for each moment of each day and for all the blessings in your life. The media heighten our fears with doomsday and horror stories of the happenings around us and in the world. When we become fear-centered instead of God-centered, we panic, lose confidence, over-react, and feel vulnerable to the forces around us. Fears keep us out of balance and in a state of disharmony. Why not meet each challenge as it arises, instead of imagining the horror that could happen? Change fearful thoughts into positive thoughts that attract positive outcomes. Place your faith and truth in the ever-present light and love that is with you always, and begin each day accepting peace and joy. Join others in visualizing a world where peace and love prevail. Trust your inner wisdom and guidance from angels to protect you, your family, and country from harm.

8. *Take Responsibility for Your Actions*

The time has come for us to take responsibility for our actions. Value, respect, and appreciate each individual and the diversities of races and cultures in the world. Truly listen to the opinions of others, even though you may not agree with them. Be honest, open, and, most importantly, selfless in giving and receiving. Humanity has learned from past experience that strife, hostility, and wars often begin when we disrespect our neighbors' land, culture, beliefs and values, or display selfish competitive, judgmental, and righteous attitudes. We must think and act in the spirit of cooperation if we desire world peace.

9. *Send Light to Dispel the Darkness*

Be among the growing numbers of people seeking to express a higher level of consciousness, quality of life, and well being for human-kind. Pray and send light to dispel the darkness surrounding those misguided individuals lost in malice and hate, intent on following a path of violence. Many will fall by their own hands; others will come to see their errors and work for the common good. If each person works toward cooperatively sharing Earth's resources and abundance, the potential for obtaining peace and prosperity in the next decade will be positive. As always, justice will prevail in the end, and humanity will fulfill its destiny.

10. *See the Love of God*

See the love of God in the faces of your family, friends and neighbors, and magnify this love with your words and deeds, preparing the way for a new day on Earth. Use your inner strength to face the trials, obstacles, and challenges ahead as you experience the great shift on Earth. The energy that flows from the universe is composed of unconditional love that encompasses all peoples of Earth. Use this source to bring healing to the planet. The time has arrived for humanity to accept its spiritual nature as co-workers with Divine Source. As you do, you will feel more peaceful, loving, and joyful. Think and act from your heart-center and see the world differently, as a place of great beauty and goodness. We will experience many challenges in reaching this point in consciousness, and for most people, it will be a difficult path with many lessons.

Your Mission is Love

In closing this chapter, I remind you that our journey on Earth follows evolutionary cycles of birth to death to rebirth, and rides the tides of earthly shifts. After each ending there are always new beginnings, new adventures, and lessons to learn. Joyfully participate in the natural flow of life; connect with your inner source of light, for it is the God within that shines through you. Let your light be a beacon of love for others on their journeys. Be steadfast in your mission in life – expressing the love of God in your thoughts, word and deeds; for love is the spiritual force throughout the universe that is the divine plan for all to follow. We have been promised a new day, where fear will lose its grip on us and the dark shadows on Earth will be transformed into light. The promise is that Archangel Michael, the Lord of the Way, and his legions of angels will dispel the evil forces from earth and clear the way for peace and love to prevail. Call on the heavenly host of angels, Holy Spirit, and spiritual teachers, and masters to keep you safe and guide you to spiritual enlightenment. Remember that we were sent to Earth to prosper and to enjoy its fruits. Our earthly school experience offers great opportunities for the progression of the soul. All has been supplied for a prosperous journey, but you must choose how you will use these divine gifts. When you are God-centered in thoughts and deeds, you will always choose wisely and experience the protective light and guidance from the heavenly host.

3

THE PRESENCE OF CELESTIAL HELPERS

Angels' Guidance

Both the Old and New Testaments of the Bible provide examples of angels' guidance that encouraged individuals to follow the path that leads to enlightenment. Most major religions of the world recognize the word angels, meaning messengers. According to the writings of Dionysius, one of the Athenians, who accepted the teaching of disciples Paul, John and James, there are three hierarchies and nine choirs of angels. They are referred to as the supreme, middle, and lower, hierarchies, and include the choir of angels. Under the supreme group are Seraphim, Cherubim and Thrones, keepers of wisdom, judgement, constancy and love. The middle group includes Dominions, Virtues, and Powers, who serve as, administrators of God's will, courage, miracles, and the law of cause and effect. The lower hierarchy includes Principalities, Archangels, and Guardian Angels, who oversee religions and nations and are God's emissaries of guardianship and service (Janie Howard, *Commune with Angels*, 1992). It is said that all things flow from God through these mediating angelic ranks, and the celestial hierarchy lead us all back to God.

There are numerous accounts of angelic involvement in human affairs. For example, angels were a constant presence in Edgar Cayce's life and are referred to in his readings. At the age of thirteen, Cayce saw an angel who granted his wish to be of service to humankind. Thereafter, Cayce dedicated his life to helping people through his many readings and activities. Angels are defined in the Eckankar literature as "Beings above ordinary man who helps to serve man in many ways. They have great powers, and are quite willing to serve people who live in harmony with them" (Eckankar Dictionary, 1989).

Since the beginning of time, messages from Angels are one of the ways that God speaks to humankind. During several of Cayce's life readings, Archangel Michael would address local members of the Association of Research and Enlightenment Search for God Study Group. His messages were both supportive and challenging. One message from Archangel Michael informed those present that the world was about to enter a spiritual renaissance period, where communication with angels would not be unusual, but part of the greater plan in our awakening. (Grant, *Are We Listening to the Angels*, 1994, 49). Grant also included a massage from Archangel Michael recorded by Nancy Fullwood in 1917, an author of several books on angels. This message foretold the coming changes on earth and in human consciousness, and that a New World of beauty and harmony is even now replacing the old chaotic earth.

Angels are not completely separated from humanity. They are our constant companions in this life and our afterlives, providing guidance and loving support. Flower Newhouse, seen by many as an authority on the kingdom of angels, called angels "Anointed Emissaries of the Will toward Goodness, Wisdom, and Perfection…their invisible influence works constantly to restrain and purify evil and to awaken dormant good in all things". Her many books, classes and lectures on the subject have served to awaken many to the mission and presence of angels in our lives. Newhouse recounts that angels support the evolution and well being of planet Earth and its entirety, and safeguards our journey through life and in drawing closer to God (Newhouse, and Isaac, *Touch by Angels,* 1998).

God has not left us on Earth to struggle alone; his celestial emissaries have helped humanity throughout the ages and, are, even now, assisting us when we ask for their help. Celestial messengers and spirit guides are gifts from our Creator, guiding and encouraging us, watching over us, protecting us, and showing us the way to spiritual enlightenment and the presence of God within us. Their help comes in the form of inspirations, insights, protection, physical and emotional healing. You may also receive help in your spiritual development, relationships, life goals, and prosperity concerns.

Robert Smith, in his book, *In the Presence of Angels (1993),* identified additional roles of angels, beyond healing and spiritual guidance that angels provide, such as, exercising authority over leaders and nations, caring for the planet and all life therein, and energizing the entire solar system. Books about angels by Flower Newhouse, Robert Smith, Doreen Virtue, Barbara Mark and Trudy Griswold, and Kim O'Neill, are listed in the reference section and provide additional information on this subject.

In the Company of Angels

As the veil between our awareness of higher dimensions becomes less dense, we can expect to receive inner communication from beings on higher planes more frequently. Angels will guide us in using higher vibrational frequencies in communicating with them and realizing our full potential. Prepare to join the many throughout the world receiving telepathically and intuitively messages from angels and archangels, spiritual guides, masters, and teachers. Some of the angelic beings that are more frequently mentioned by those who telepathically channel angels include:

- **Michael**—"*He who is like God, Lord of the Way:*" - Releases us from fear, battles evil, brings courage, is the angel of change, the supreme protector and guardian of Earth.
- **Gabriel**—"*God is my strength:*" Angel of Paradise, Resurrection".
- **Rafael**—"*God heals:*" – Source of all healing, and divinely inspires artists, aids travelers.
- **Uriel**—"*Light of God:*" – Associated with our future and goals, transforms misfortune into great advantages.

- **Asriel**—*"Angel of Death:"* – Help for those crossing over to the other side of the veil.
- **Raguel**—*"Angel of Luminaries:"*– radiates inspiration and mystical experience, guardian of our seven – Chakras.
- **Metatron**—*"Lord of Light:"* –the ray of Earth's ascension, and protector of the planet.
- **Angels of Destiny**—*"Watcher angels:"*-watches over and protects all from birth into adulthood and helps us awaken to the presence of God.
- **Guardian Angels:** - establish a continuing partnership with us throughout life. Angels respond to our calls for help and guidance, providing loving support and protection. As a constant companion, Guardian Angels intervene when we are in danger and commune with us in many ways to increase our spiritual wellbeing. They daily and nightly instruct us to help open awareness of the presence of God within and our destiny in life (Flower and Isaac 1998), Grant (2005), Virtue (1997) and lecture notes.

Of course, there are many more angels helping the planet and its inhabitants. Flower Newhouse describes in detail the kingdom of angels, in *Touched by Angels*, and referred to angels as extraordinary beings who have been given the responsibility to be an extension of their Creator, maintaining order and assuring progress throughout the universe. She describes four great waves, or grouping of angels serving our planet. One of these, the nature kingdom, is seldom directly involved with human evolution.

The other three groups are the Angels that are serving the Lord Christ, Angels serving the Holy Spirit, and Angels of Destiny. Angels serving the Lord Christ work to lift the consciousness of all humanity Godward through worship, healing and prayer. Angels serving the Holy Spirit work to awaken inspire and enlighten humanity in all aspects of life. The Angels of Destiny work with AKashic Records, our life plans and individual Karma, in their roles as Guardian Angels (*Touched by Angels 1998, 27*).

ECK Living Master, Sri Harold Klemp, also reports that sometimes these angels appear physically to us during a life threatening episode, and then disappear before we can give thanks. Other times, they may be accompanied by blue or white light as a sign of their presence, and appear in an inner vision or dream.

Be ever mindful that you also can be a channel/messenger for angelic guidance, by living the motto - "Even as you have blessed me, so may I be a channel for a blessing to others".

Angels' Messages

You are changing, Dear Ones, to be more like us in the heavenly domains. Believe It. Changes are taking place in your inner thoughts and your inner desires for enlightenment. Listen for our angelic guidance and while in restful repose, envision with us: A world where all peoples of the earth remember their true divine nature and express these truths in their daily lives. A world where humankind has ascended in thoughts and deeds to higher frequencies of love, compassion, harmony, and unity, and while remaining in physical form, experience - The kingdom of Heaven on Earth.

Dear Ones, we ask that you reflect on the following questions. Why are you so involved in fighting each other when you are one family in the eyes of your Creator? Why are you so intent on thinking you are right and your brother is wrong? Why do you do so much destruction to your earthly home, yourselves and those around you? Have you not learned, through lifetime after lifetimes, that the destructive activities you perpetrate only bring on more destruction? Why is it so difficult for you to express your true nature of compassionate love for one and another?

Dear Brothers and Sisters, turn your intentions on saving all life on the planet. Lift your thoughts to the celestial realms and pray for forgiveness and enlightenment. You cannot enter the kingdom of heaven until you lay down your arms and embrace your brothers and sisters with love, peace, and compassion. This is the way to your salvation and that of the world. As you extend love to all humankind - so shall

you receive love more abundantly. Allow
Divine Spirit within you to show you the
way.

Spiritual Helpers As Co-Workers

Even now, Earth is shifting to a higher vibrational frequency. There are those who have moved to higher levels
of consciousness in their spiritual quest, and are working to improve the quality of life and well-being for all
humanity on the planet. We are asked to send loving
light to those misguided souls, whose malice, destructive
behaviors, and non-peaceful coexistence have led them
astray. Pray for those entrenched in errors, and pray to dispel the darkness in the world. Know that divine order will
prevail and humanity will fulfill its destiny. The struggle
to bring light to all receptive hearts is winning the day, for
humanity is ascending to the consciousness of love, peace
and harmony. We are told to keep the faith, keep peace,
and love in our hearts, and demonstrate the Divine Truth
of God's Love in our lives. This we can do, for we have
the support and blessings of higher spiritual and celestial
beings.

An assembly of great masters, those living and those
ascended to higher planes, are joining spirit guides, angels,
and the returned of great avatars and teachers of past ages
to prepare humankind for this great leap forward. Many
have waited for this evolutional cycle in human advancement that is now unfolding before us. The powerful forces
of higher frequencies at work on Earth and in the universe
are aligned with cosmic evolutional minor and major
cycles that occur every 12,000 years and 144,000 years.

These cycles produce transformational advancement for humanity, on the spiritual, emotional, mental and physical levels. Cosmic cycles also coincide with major geologic shifts and climate changes on the planet. You are living witnesses to universal and natural laws in action, during this major evolutionary period on Earth. Many departed souls have returned to Earth to participate in and support this great – leap – forward for humankind and the lower material planes in the universe. Therefore, be at peace and know that all is working in Divine Order.

The next chapter addresses the process of soul's departure from the material body at the moment of death and its passage to higher planes. In addition, a descriptive account of soul's ascension to higher planes, and examples of afterlife experiences may help many to release the fear of death, with reassurance that the soul lives on in full consciousness.

4

SOULS' ASCENSION
TO HIGHER PLANES

Eliminating the Fear of Dying

Some people will choose to make their transition during these times of Earth changes, rather than experience the hardship and challenges that will follow. Those who are old, frail, ill, and otherwise incapacitated, will die from natural causes, thus completing their life cycles, and departing at their individually appointed times. Others will be killed in war, terrorist attacks, untimely accidents, and catastrophic events, leaving before their times.

Feelings of being unlovable, inadequate, abused, or melancholy, can also make a person long for an early death before their appointed time. On the other hand, the fear of death often delays our departure when we are not willing to mentally or physically release earthly attachments. Bargaining to delay death when the time arrives makes the process more difficult for the soul-self to release itself from the body. The time to rejoice is when you naturally approach the completion of another life cycle on Earth, and make preparation to ascend in a finer body to a higher plane to continue your soul's journey. Death will lose its sting when we learn to accept death as a joyful graduation and passage from this earthly plane to a rebirth on higher planes of life.

Dr. John Hefferlin described death as the transition beyond this three-dimensional world into other worlds of varying dimensions, and into an ever-expanding universe with ever-broadening horizons. He states, "We die, but we live! Life, as we know it in this three-dimensional world, will continue just so long as the body retains sufficient channels through which the vital energy of God can flow. When enough of these channels cease to function, the body dies. It is like discarding old clothes." (*Dimensions of Life Beyond Life, Science of Mind-booklet*).

Consider that death and rebirth are different sides of the same coin. The front side is the entrance of the soul into the material world, and the back side is the soul's departure from the physical body and return journey to the spirit realms. At both ends of the birth and death cycles, there is joyous anticipation, as the soul's family group receives and guides the returning soul for the next phase of its journey, be it heavenly or earthly. Birth and death represent universal laws operating in repeated cycles of incarnation to incarnation.

According to several books on the afterlife (see reference list), there are many dimensional planes or realms of consciousness that exist for our souls' expression after death. There are also diverse human states of consciousness on these planes. We are attracted to a dimension of like souls who share our beliefs. If we express a lower thought pattern of greed, jealousy, and malice toward others here on Earth, we will surely occupy a lower thought plane with like-minded souls in heaven, for the Law of Attraction is constantly playing out, both on Earth and in heaven. Ernest Holmes, author, *The Science of Mind* and other books, explains how the law of attraction works on the mental level. According to Holmes (1998), "a thought atmosphere surrounds every person and is the result of our conscious and unconscious thought patterns. In turn, our thoughts become the reason for and the cause of all that comes into our life. We are either attracting or repelling, for like attracts like" (294).

Consider what you are attracting in your life - is it for your highest good? Consider why you attracted some people and repel others. Could it be that you are projecting either negative or positive thoughts to which others react? A good exercise is to examine how the law of attraction plays out in your life and what thought patterns you are projecting into the world. If your thoughts are attracting more undesirable things, then change what your thoughts dwell on and fill your mind with positive and loving thoughts and experiences.

When Transition Occurs

At death, our angels guide us to that perfect place where souls gain new insights and lessons needed to progress to higher spiritual planes. Our minds remain active and our personality intact as we leave our physical form behind.

I am told that there is no interruption of our conscious awareness when we move to our next experience in the spirit realms and assume the finer astral and soul body. A life review of our recent earth life enables us to select those experiences in the higher realms needed for advancing our soul's growth. Chaney's description of the afterlife in *The Mystery of Death & Dying*, 1989, encouraged us to:

"Look to the light, Seeker! Look to death as life's highest adventure. Look to death as the soul's greatest hope for initiation—the soul's ultimate union with God. So live when that moment of opportunity approaches, the portals of paradise open wide, and a voice from the Clear Light will bid you entrance: 'Well done, good and faithful servant. Enter now into the joys of eternal life" (142).

The following description of the dying process may help to clarify what occurs in the physical body at the moment of death, and soul's ascension to higher planes. With the aid of hypnotherapy/past life regression, a few individuals are able to recall their past deaths and passage to higher realms, however as we advance spiritually, memories of our ascension at death will become common place. The soul, is said to be the seat of memory, and already contains a record of everything that has ever happened to us. Alice Bailey, the well-known author of *Esoteric Healing*, along with Chaney, Flowers, Fox, Heindel, Spencer, and Holmes, have described this journey in some detail. The following summarization of the major points of the soul's departure from its physical body is based on the writings of Bailey and Chaney.

Let us begin at the moment of death as we depart from our physical body. It has been observed that the ego, or spirit/soul self, withdraws from the body by way of the head, heart, or sometimes the solar plexus, based on one's highest level of self-consciousness. The soul essence, which is made up of the mind and the life force contained within the body, also withdraws, at which time the silver cord (which united the higher self to the lower body) snaps. It also is reported that the process of withdrawal of the soul/spirit-self or ego, observed by medical personnel and family members around the bedside of the dying person, may take from ten to thirty minutes or slightly longer. When there is a soft light in the room, the aura (a light around the body) of the deceased will be seen to extend gradually from the body and than rise out and above the body. Within five to twenty minutes it is usually separated from the body, hovering horizontally above the body before it vanishes out of sight. However, in some cases the hazy light of the person's aura may remain in the room for several hours or days after the person is pronounced dead.

A personal description of this process is described in Dr. Kenneth Ring's book, *Life at Death*, 1980, 226) in which Estelle describes her husband's transition when seeing his spirit leave the body as it emerged from his head and gradually molded itself into the replica of his earth-body. She saw it remained suspended about a foot above his body, lying in the same position, horizontal and attached by a cord to the head. Then the cord broke and the spirit-form floated away, passing through the wall.

Those who have observed the death process are reminded of the similarity to the birth process. We observe this with the delivery of a newborn baby attached to its mother by the umbilical cord. When the cord is severed, the baby is freed and begins its earthly life. The cycle of birth and death is consistent with the universal laws of nature. Bailey speaks of this as a part of the Great Illusion, which only exists because of the veils we have gathered around ourselves. Some speak of death as passing through a doorway or hallway into another room (dimension) that leads to our true heavenly home. We remain in the higher realms/dimensions/planes (some call it heaven) until incarnating to earth again to experience physical life in a dense body again for a designated time period, that is determined by higher spiritual laws.

According to Bailey, the soul is seated in the heart and departs from the physical body with the loss of consciousness. She uses terms that the average reader may not be familiar with, such as, the "etheric" body, described as the inner "substantial" form upon which the physical body is built. Further consideration is given to Bailey's description about the physiological changes in the body when death occurs (*Esoteric Healing*, 1980).

At the appointed time, the soul sounds a "word of withdrawal" from its own plane and immediately an interior process and reaction occurs in the person. These physical events (in connection with the heart and affecting the blood stream, and the nervous system and endocrine system) bring about the pathological predisposition to death. Next, a vibration runs along the "Nadis" (which are the etheric counterpart of the entire nervous system that underlies every single nerve in the entire physical body) and responds to the sound/word to withdraw. This signals the soul to organize and detach from the body. As a result, the blood stream is changed, the glands inject a substance into the bloodstream that affects the heart and creates a reflex action in the brain. (This substance is one of the basic causes of coma and loss of consciousness.) When the psychic tremor (body vibration) occurs, the effect is loosening or breaking the connection between the threads-of-life force/Nadis and nervous system, detaching the etheric body from its dense covering. This detachment is often observed in the eyes and peaceful repose of the dying.

Following this process, the organized etheric body gathers itself, beginning with the extremities and organs, in preparation for its final exit from the physical body. This has been called the "death pull." There may be a pause of events as these processes take place in the body. The etheric body emerges from the dense physical body in gradual stages at the chosen point of exit (head or heart), and after a brief period is gradually dispersed above the body before it vanishes.

You will not find an explanation in medical texts regarding the dying process and soul departure. An understanding of the physical changes in the body during the moment of transition can reduce some of our fears. As a hospice volunteer witnessing bedside deaths, and those of family members, I have observed the changes in the physical body during the time of the soul departure, including the blue, or colorless extremities, and rapid decline in organ function. If drugs are not administered to disturb the process, the approach of death can be a peaceful and sacred moment.

While the physical signs of death are occurring there is also spiritual passage of the soul at death, reported by Flower Newhouse and Stephen Isaac. They state that "at that moment the Angels of Death administer an electrical force which severs the inner bodies from the physical form and brings about the condition known as death. The first awareness that the soul has is an engulfing Light, and the wonderfully compassionate Archangel of Transition, of great beauty and love, who welcomes you back to your heavenly home" (118).

Seeing the Light

Earlyne Chaney, *The Mystery of Death and Dy*ing, also states that "every soul, aware or unaware witnesses the dawning of the "Clear Light of the Void," prior to the moment of leaving the physical body at death" (1989, 43). The Clear Light is defined as the reflection of consciousness devoid of darkness and all limitations. Chaney refers to it "as a purified perfection shining like a dazzling sun upon the mirror of your mind, as your consciousness passes from the limitations of the brain to expanded awareness". She adds, "At the moment of death we merge with the "Clear Light of the Void" through which we are released from our karmic "sins." (47).

However, if we miss the Clear Light at the point of death, she states that "there is the opportunity to see the "Secondary Light," less dazzling or bright than the first, but fully visible a half-hour after clinical death. According to Chaney, this is the point when the heart seed atoms – containing the record of our total past, including the physical, emotional and mental aspects, and the astral form and silver cord – are released from the physical body. The newly born spiritual form may depart immediately with the cessation of the heartbeat, or linger as the astral form gains its new body. Furthermore, we are told that the Secondary Light does not dawn until about half an hour after the heart seed atom departs and the silver cord breaks, signaling final death.

Chaney explains that "the void" is like the center of nothingness because it is beyond description; however the Clear Light of the Void is coming face to face with God –in the form of the light of lights. It may require one to fifteen hours for the release of soul and seed atoms. She stipulates that embalming, burial or cremation should not take place for a period of three days following death. It is better to place the body in a refrigerated locker for those days while the soul is experiencing the journey of the after-death state, which includes a journey into self-understanding.

The fear of dying can be reduced when we fully understand the process of the soul's departure from the physical form. Death can be viewed as leaving one room and passing into another more beautiful room, or exchanging our outer garment for one more accommodating to our new status. We still retain our uniqueness, personality, and memories in the afterlife, so what is there to fear? Death is preordained and when our time on Earth is completed, the dying process proceeds in an orderly timeless fashion. The release of the soul – personality from its confined physical form and ascension to higher planes – is automatic and effortless. This is the time to finally let go of all material attachments and let the nature and divine order fulfill its mission. We know that the Angel-of-Death and our guardian angels are there to guide us safely home, for many on their deathbed have spoken of their presence.

Positive Presence for the Dying

Let us therefore accept death as a natural completion of our earthly journeys, and feel peaceful in releasing loved ones who are in various stages of their transition. Whenever possible, be at the bedside of your loved ones in a quiet and peaceful state of mind. Even when the person is unconscious, you can softly remind them to focus on the Clear Light and the presence of angels guiding them to their heavenly home and departed loved ones. Avoid lamentation, loud talking, and other distractions in the room when the dying person is in a coma, so the person in transition can focus on the Clear Light. It is also important that the last thought of the dying be peaceful and positive. Any interruptions will interfere with the person experiencing the "bardo" – the after death journey of the soul on its way to higher realms, and seeing their life pass before them in a flash, beginning from present time back to birth. During this time remain quiet and prayerful. The body should not be disturbed or moved in the final stages of death. Family members may recite the Lord's Prayer, Rosary, or the person's favorite prayers and scriptures, chant softly sacred sounds – OM, AUM, and HU, or play sounds of harp, or classical string music.

We often hold our loved ones to the earthly plane when we continue to grieve their loss for long periods of time, for they will stay close to us to try to alleviate our grief. This will delay their enjoyment and progress in the afterlife. It is better to project uplifting and cheerful thoughts and pray for their spiritual progress and well being. Celebrate their graduation from this life and passage to their next experience. Surround them with your love and then release them to the divine light and love of God. After several weeks have passed, you may feel their comforting presence and desire to communicate with them in your prayers and dreams.

Sudden death, from an accident, stroke, heart attack, or in combat situations can occur so swiftly that the person initially may not realize that they have left their physical body. Family members may feel the presence of their spirits, or have dreams that they need help in understanding what has happened to them. When praying for the dead, you can tell them they have departed from their physical form and have moved into a new reality. Call on their angels to guide them to their heavenly home and surround them in divine light. Continue your prayers for the departed, for they hear our prayers and benefit greatly from them. In time, as we become more spiritually enlightened, the illusion of death will be seen as a welcome return to our spiritual home.

There is much that is not known about the higher spiritual planes. At the present time, the veil between these planes and the earth's atmosphere remains closed, and our conscious awareness and memories of past life journeys are limited. However, in time, as we evolve to higher levels of spiritual enlightenment, more information will be forthcoming as to life on these planes. The following angel message gives us a glimpse of the higher realms.

Angel's Message

*Many beings inhabit the spiritual realms;
some with bodies similar to our earthly
bodies, but lighter. Those entities on the
highest levels are formless and of the purest
consciousness of light and love. Their
souls extend light, love, and the God-
Consciousness throughout the universe.
The spiritual realms have many levels,
dimensions, densities, and forms. A soul
can move within and between these
levels as its consciousness and spiritual
development allows. At death, we take
our personality and beliefs with us and
continue to express, create, experience,
and expand our awareness in progressive
stages to higher levels of refinement and
wisdom. In time, the self merges with the
Great Divine Source, where it becomes one
with the Creative Mind and obtains God
–Realization. Each soul progresses at its
own rate in the higher planes and, with the
help of spiritual guides, selects experiences
beneficial for the soul's progression and
learning. Personalities holding rigid beliefs
about the afterlife, heaven, or hell, could
impede one's progress in higher planes, for
entities create their own conditions and
experiences based on their beliefs and
thought patterns.*

Passage to Higher Planes

Mark Macy's report entitled, *The Various Realms of Spirit Worlds,* 2002, described the after-physical-death ascension path to the spirit realms. It seems that after we leave the earth's dense, slow-vibrating matter and energy, we enter the quantum realm using our etheric body. The report describes this buffer zone between the physical and astral worlds as a place to readjust to a lighter subtler and more vibrant body, and to release past-life issues. The astral realm is a place of form and structure like Earth, but more adaptable to thoughts and intentions. Macy suggests that most people from our physical plane are residents here in lighter and finer astral and mental light bodies. This realm is often referred to as paradise or summerland and has many divisions of varying vibratory rates, where thoughts create one's reality.

The higher ethereal or soul planes are described as formless worlds consisting of beings of pure consciousness and divine inspiration. The various dimensions described in these realms are often referred to as mental-causal, celestial, and cosmic. These planes are considered the home of ascended masters and spiritual entities with light bodies, and are where the spirit and soul will merge with the Divine Source to become beams of light. Furthermore, he states that we are multidimensional beings containing a series of finer bodies housing our soul that are shed at appropriate times during our ascension to higher realms of existence.

Sri Harold Klemp, The Mahanta, and ECK Living Master, lists the planes that souls ascend to beginning with the Physical/body, Astral/emotional, Causal/

Memory, Mental/mind, and Etheric/unconscious planes. Above these are the pure positive worlds of spirit. The Living ECK Master is the title of the spiritual leader of ECKANKAR. His duty is to lead Souls back to God.

Adding to this information is Jane Roberts's book *Seth Speaks* (1983), in which she channeled Seth, a multi-dimensional personality no longer in physical reality. Seth describes the unlimited varieties of experiences, according to our development, that await us in the afterlife. The book recounts the three main choices one has in the afterlife:

1. Reincarnate to Earth again to focus on making corrections to a past life or use it as the basis for new experiences.
2. Choose another system of probability (dimension) quite different from the past life, such as another planetary experience other than Earth.
3. Choose an in-between rest stage before making a choice. An entity may remain in this rest stage for some time, until ready to move forward for another experience for the soul's development.

Information I received from spirit guides, angels, and souls in other realms describes the higher planes as pure consciousness and light. Each plane of consciousness has its own qualities. The level above our earth plane has the focus of thought energy, which allows inhabitants to direct their thoughts to learn lessons of openness, truth, love, and creativity, and to manifest what is desired. Here, reality is manifested and maintained by thought. There is no attachment to that which is manifested, and after it serves its purpose, it is dissolved by thought.

Sri Harold Klemp reminds us that lower planes are a material realm of time, matter, space, and energy; whereas the higher planes (the true world of God) are that area beyond time and space. Klemp refers to the Physical Plane as a place of unique opportunity for growth and a testing ground of the Soul. The Astral Plane, a higher side of the Physical Plane, is the source of emotion and feeling and resembles places on the physical plane in a highly refined form. Next is the Causal Plane, the source of memories of past lives on the lower planes. Above this is the Mental Plane, the home of many inhabitants with high mental development who are preparing to become Co-workers with God. The Etheric Plane lies just beyond, and is a higher aspect of the Mental Plane. It is the seat of intuition, source of unconscious mind, where all dreams begin. It acts as a buffer between spirit worlds above and the material worlds below. Above these planes are the Soul Planes, the first of the true spiritual worlds where Souls reach the state of Self-Realization and experience the pure Sound and Light of God as they become Co-workers with God (*The Easy Way Discourses* 1992, 22).

The Question of Suicide and Karma

The question has been raised, on numerous occasions, as to what happens to those who prematurely end their life by suicide. The majority of such individuals who take their own lives are usually in great mental and/or physical distress, and not morally responsible for their behavior at the time. In late life, the desire to end the pain, lengthy period of suffering, loved ones burden of care giving, and depression and loneliness, is often the driving force in the act of suicide. Teenage suicide is often committed for reasons of personal rejection, lack of love, and under-standing and acceptance from significant people in their life. Emotional and mental distress, including feelings of failure, separation, and hopelessness can be other pre-cipitating factors for suicide. These individuals enter the afterlife in a confused mental/emotional state and need our prayers for forgiveness and love.

Chaney is of the opinion that those who die by violent accident go through the same process of the soul depar-ture from the body described earlier. However, those who commit suicide interrupt the cosmic timing of their nat-ural death cycles of soul's departure from the earthly life, and therefore create karmic consequences for their suicidal act. Their souls are held captive to the Earth plane, near loved ones and the people they have deserted. They will owe a debt of karmic service to these individuals on earth for the length of time they would have been incarnated in the physical body. After fulfilling their cosmic death cycle (the natural timing for their soul's departure from earth) the soul is released to progress to higher planes according to its karmic destiny. Chaney adds that during this time the soul is held near to those still on earth, it must per-form service to help the grief stricken family and friends through their life journeys. In most cases, the departed soul must reincarnate to fulfill karmic obligations and revisit the same problems it attempted to escape by the act of suicide. The departed soul has an obligation to its soul group (those who incarnate together and form specific relationships and fulfill specific supportive roles) in the group's lost opportunity to fulfill their karmic destiny of service, growth and learning.

The term Karma refers to the cause and effect of individual actions. Karma, is not punishment, it is only a natural consequence in a lesson to be learned. Nature does not punish, it only teaches us when we err in fulfilling our destiny and service to others, or disrupt the natural timing and cosmic flow of life. In the afterlife, or interlife planes, the soul will have the opportunity to review, assess and learn from its past life experiences and plan for its next incarnation on earth. According to Paul Twitchell, Ascended ECK Master, we are constantly creating Karma or debts, during our earthly journey that eventually must be paid off. The first type is the Karma of fate, earned in a previous lifetime, and must be paid off in another lifetime. The second type is reserve Karma, will be met at the time and place that the Lord of Karma designates. The third type of Karma, is the daily Karma individuals make day to day during each lifetime. (*Twitchell, Letters to Gail, 1978,162*)

Is There Proof of an Afterlife?

Science has advanced to a point where direct communication with deceased love ones and friends is now possible using radio, telephone, television, and a combination of communication technologies. We can now say our loved ones are only a telephone call away and mean it. This technology is discussed in Theo Locher and Maggy Harsch-Fischbach, *Breakthroughs in Technical Spirit Communication 1997,* and Pat Kubis and Mark

Macy, *Conversations Beyond* the *Light* 1995. The authors describe this technology in its early stages of development in the following way:

"A new science is being born - the science of Instrumental Transcommunication (ITC). Today, using high-tech communication, the "dead" are now transmitting information to our scientists in pictures, text, and voice via television screens, computers, and telephones. Now, a "deceased" scientist can speak via television to a roomful of scientists on earth." (Kubis and Macy 1995).

Both the *Transdimension Journal* (1999, vol. 2) and also the book, *Conversations Beyond the Light*, (Kubis and Macy 1995) describe communication across dimensions in detail. A brief list follows of the accomplishments reported by ITC researchers over the past decade.

- First audible dialogue across dimensions through the Spircom Device developed by American researcher George Meek.
- Heavenly chorus that emerged from the radios of Italian experimenter Marcello Bacci.
- Whispery voices of nature spirits reporting through the German experimenter Fredrich Malkoff.
- Picture of departed ITC experimenters delivered through the television of German experimenter Adolf Homes.
- Messages from departed loved ones captured on audio-tape and computer sent to grieving family members.
- A three-page letter to French ITC researchers written by Jules Verne, a century after his death, deliv-

ered through fax machine to Luxembourg experimenters Maggy and Jules Harsch-Fischback.

- Pictures of spirit-world landscapes through televisions and computers of the same Luxembourg experimenters and many others. (1999, 27).

This may seem unbelievable to the average person, but our communication technology and experimenters on Earth, in collaboration with researchers in the afterlife, have made this link possible.

The researchers in the afterlife seem to reside on the mid-third Astral Plane, where most humans are said to go after death. This plane is said to be most like Earth, located on what researchers called the planet Marduk, which is outside of Earth's solar system. The vivid description of this plane and those of the fourth, fifth, six, and seventh planes was provided by those in the spirit world, and also individual astral travelers. For the first time, we have a road map of the soul's journey after physical death. Messages sent to ITC scientists, from those on the planet Marduk, describe the incredible beauty of the mid-astral plane as a safe and loving environment where health and happiness prevails. You join loved ones and friends, not only from your most recent life on Earth, but also other past lives residing on this plane. We are told that some people remain on the mid-astral plane for hundreds of years, while others choose to reincarnate to Earth or advance to higher planes.

The computer images that ITC received from this plane are illustrated in Kubis and Macy's and Locher and Harsch-Fischbach's books. These pictures provided verification to family members still on earth of loved ones continued lives. If you are curious about what to expect in these higher realms, I suggest you read the books cited above, and ITC scientists' latest reports on their websites. Hopefully, their reports will help many to gain a healthier and more joyful perspective of continued life journeys on the astral and higher planes, as more published information becomes available.

Angels' Visions of the Astral Plane

I was surprised that telepathic messages from my angels describing the astral planes were similar to ITC reports. My angels provided me with the following description of the plane we aspire to after physical death:

Angel Message

There is much love and joy on this conscious plane, with many communities and beings living together, sharing similar interests, activities, and friendships. This plane also has a vast diversity of life forms, including plants, animals, fowl and sea life. Angels and higher spiritual beings dwell lovingly together with entities.

The beauty on this plane is beyond description, with plants and other creatures expressing their own loving, spiritual essence. The light shines through all, giving off beautiful colors that reflect the inner spirit of all life. This location contains great halls of learning, libraries, concert halls, artistic creation, and architecturally pleasing buildings.

Transporting oneself from place to place is by thought projection to the desired location, or air, land, and water vehicles. This is a plane of creative thought where all is possible; therefore, all things within natural laws can be manifested. The air on this plane has a life-giving essence that allows one to breathe in all that is needed to support the finer energy body without the need for nourishment as on Earth.

All life forms are preserved and never consumed here. Darkness does not occur as on Earth, for all is light here. The light from the rising, midday, and evening suns provides a constant glow of beautiful and varied colors and shades, with plants adding their own softly glowing and inner lights and colors.

Can we begin now to prepare for our transition to higher planes of consciousness by using the process of creative thought and soul travel? The answer is yes, although it will take some practice, especially for individuals who find it difficult to control their random thoughts. Unfocused and emotionally charged thoughts create purposeless, random acts, confusion, and stagnation on higher planes. On these planes thoughts create and manifest what is, and therefore require a steadfast state of mindfulness, peace-fulness, and focused intention. Loving thoughts are the motivating forces that manifest desires on higher planes. Ones' thoughts are readily known and observable and serve as the method for communication and manifesting on higher planes.

Mark Macy's article in *Transdimension Journal,* enti-tled *"The Bridge to the World Beyond,"* arrives at the same conclusions in the use of thought on higher planes in affirming that:

"In our physical universe we regard forces such as grav-ity, momentum, and thrust to be responsible for moving objects in time and space. What is the force that provides movement in the subtler dimensions? I believe it is desire and intent. When spirit friends talk about meeting with higher beings to learn methods of spiritual advancement, what they are actually learning are methods of focusing their desires and intentions not- not just allowing distract-ing thoughts to clutter their minds as they do for us here on Earth. Spiritual masters here on Earth have been teach-ing spiritual aspirants the same thing for centuries. The key to spiritual ascension is to clear the mind of random thoughts and to focus" (1999, 218).

Additional Considerations

Therefore, I would recommend that you begin now to clear your mind now of all hateful, angry, resentful thoughts and material attachments that would bind you to the earth's plane. Become God-centered instead of self-centered. Focus your intention and desires on all that is good in the world, be at peace with your fellow human beings and reflect on the following statements by Elsie Sechrist:

1. First, not only is the afterlife a certainty, but the veil between physical and nonphysical life is not as impenetrable as many people have thought.
2. Second, life, learning, and growth are just as much a part of our experience in the hereafter as it is in this material life.
3. God's infinite, healing love is always available to us, whether we are here on earth or in the spirit world.
4. The continuity of life is a gift from our loving Father-Mother.
5. God's creation is an orderly and purposeful Universe, in which the Law of Love is supreme (1992, 273).

In this respect, let us consider our afterlives as a continuation of all our earthly lives, and that each passage on earth offers unique learning opportunities and choices for the progression of the soul's personality. Your soul's journey in the now and the hereafter is one continuous experience divided in time periods and locations. During the hereafter phase, you are able to revitalize and assimilate previous learning before proceeding to your next phase on earth, or another plane. You would be bored-to-death, worn-out, stagnated, and unable to create new possibilities for growth if you remained a thousand or more years in one location, such as earth. We all need periodic breaks to refresh our spirit, mind and body, and to assimilate past experiences before continuing our cosmic journeys that lead us back to a reunion with our creator. Remember, it is the totality of life experiences in the continuous now that is most meaningful for the soul's growth.

Chapter 5 continues the discussion on the roles of angels and higher beings in our lives, and offers steps on how you can begin the communication process with your angels, spiritual guides, and deceased loved ones.

5

CONNECTING WITH ANGELS AND LOVED ONES

Communication with Angels

As our consciousness ascends, we will find ourselves communicating more with celestial beings, including angels, spirit guides, a host of ascended masters, and other spiritual beings. We are all blessed by having guardian angels with us from birth to death and beyond. They prepare the way for our earthly progress and remain with us until we depart from this plane. Newhouse and Isaac inform us that Guardian Angels are always feminine (1998, 53). They send us impressions, intuitive insights, and inner promptings that protect us from danger, and encourage us to take the next steps in our spiritual growth. They never interfere with our free will, for we always have the choice to accept or reject their guidance.

Angels, archangels, and a hierarchy of heavenly hosts are said to assist our Divine Creator in managing the vast cosmos, and are present on all dimensions, planes and realms of life. We are told that each person has at least two guardian angels that lovingly offer support and aid whenever we seek their help. Some individuals are able to visualize their angels; many have felt the presence of their angels, and now, more than ever, many are actively communicating with their angels. Angels are involved in our lives during birth, death, illness, grief, crisis, and in times of danger. Ask your angel for advice, guidance, protection or assistance, for they do not intervene in our lives unless we request their help. Listen for their response and pay attention when they alert you to approaching danger or situations that need quick resolution.

There are stories about angels in human form coming to the aid of people in difficult situations, and then quickly vanishing before receiving thanks were given. Those who have experienced the presence of angels report that their countenances are peaceful, loving, caring, and supportive. Their love is unconditional, comprehensive, and considerate of our needs. There is no time or place where angels are not around us, available for any requests and eager to let us know of their presence when we are open and receptive.

I have always been an avid reader of metaphysical and inspirational books, especially during times of stress, loss and grief. However, books about angels were not included in my personal library until the passing of my dear sister. I began noticing such books in bookstores, as if the angels were trying to get my attention. I received great comfort and peace of mind after reading several books about angel communication, and also after attending several workshops on the subject.

Since my first joyful contact with angels, I have maintained telepathic communication with angels on a regular basis, receiving a wealth of helpful information and guidance. The following steps in angel communication have worked well for me; however it is best to practice and discover what works for you in receiving angels' guidance. For beginners, the following steps may enable you to be receptive in receiving messages from angels and heavenly spirits.

1. Clear your mind of all distracting thoughts and clutter, and focus your intention on making contact with your angel companions.
2. Write down your questions and concerns prior to asking for assistance. This will help you to focus your thoughts and clearly identify your concerns.
3. Maintain a peaceful state of mind and breathe slowly and deeply throughout your contact. You may find it is helpful to visualize yourself surrounded by a large round or oval bubble of protective and loving light. Breathe into your light bubble and enlarge it to surround your body and the entire room.
4. You may wish to begin with a short prayer or affirmation, such as: "I am deeply grateful for the loving presence of angels in my life, for they are always available for support and guidance when I ask. "I now seek your advice, guidance, instruc-

tion, and support. Speak to me now Loving angels!"

5. Wait patiently and you will receive intuitively or telepathically a soft voice greeting you by name with "Yes, we are here dear one." This may be followed by a short message. State your questions out loud one at a time and listen carefully and patiently for a response. In the beginning their voices may be soft, and their responses slow in coming. However, continue to be attentive and patiently wait for a response.

6. Don't be discouraged if at first you are not successful, just relax and breathe deeply to improve the reception. Holding your breath, feeling anxious, and background noise will prevent a clear reception. If the reception is poor, try again another time or day. Mornings and evening hours are better for me than afternoon hours.

7. You may hear the angel's voice telepathically in you right inner ear, or see in your inner mind's eye images of words, or symbols that convey the message. Expect to receive a clear and concise message that addresses your specific concerns. With practice, you will eventually be able to carry on a normal conversation with your angels.

8. After the message is received, thank your angels and express your gratitude for their guidance. In many cases, more than one angel may respond to your requests. Acknowledge all by their names, if this has been given to you.

9. Read what you wrote without judgment, and carefully consider any guidance received. Angels' messages may be informational, supportive, instructional, or a combination of all three.

Even if you do not agree with the advice or guidance received, all should be taken seriously. When you ask the date that an event will occur in your life, their response concerning time is usually vague. Celestial time is the eternal now that includes present and future potentials, a continuous circular process, not our current linear view of time. Angels see probable events occurring if you continue on the current path. However, we can freely choose a different path, which will usually change the anticipated outcome of an event or situation.

Angels will alert us to potential danger and unsafe life choices, which gives us a window of opportunity to take preventive action or change our direction. Angels have a long view of life on Earth and see our present decisions leading to future possibilities and outcomes. Consequently, thoughts, decisions or actions already set in motion will be manifested unless they are intercepted or canceled with a different thought, decision, or action. The following are examples of angels' messages that I received that reassure humanity of their constant presence in our lives.

Angels' Message

> *Dear Ones, we are here. We come to you in love. We bless your work for peace on Earth. Now that the veil of consciousness*

has become more transparent, our message is coming through to many. No preparation is needed to receive our messages, just listen to what flows intuitively or telepathically to you. You see, God's helpers are ever present, as it was in the beginning, so it is now and forever will be. You are the very essence of God's Beingness and can talk with God and hear His voice at any time. In fact, your higher consciousness does this continuously. Your higher consciousness is your soul, which is inter-dimensional, and divinely connected to the Creator. When you accept your divinity, you will become a true companion with the Creator.

Dear Ones, you are blessed. We want to work with you on your earthly mission to bring love and peaceful solutions to the world's problems. Do this by offering unconditional love to each person, listen with a compassionate and an understanding heart to opinions and suggestions, and appreciating the contributions offered for world peace. Reassure those with fear and doubt that peace will prevail in the end, for it is divinely ordained and is even now being manifested on the planet. We now bid thee farewell with our love and blessings.

Many have proclaimed the rewards in communicating with angels, resulting in a more positive, productive, and harmonious life. The authors below tell us more about these rewards.

"Angels work with our souls, in conjunction with Universal Mind, to help us raise our sights and spirits by reminding us of the truth, beauty, and goodness that exists within everything. By invoking our angels to help us accomplish mundane as well as inspired tasks, we can be confident that all will proceed according to Higher Will, not just ours alone. Through this act of cooperation, we lose our sense of isolation. We truly comprehend that we are not alone, nor unaided. There is help and guidance all around us when we start opening to the state in which miracles can occur. (Alma Daniel, Timothy Wyllie, and Andrew Ramer" (*Ask Your Angels*, 6).

Communications Across the Veil

The spirits of our deceased loved ones remain in our thoughts. We often feel their presence, telepathically hear them call our name, or give words of comfort. The love we shared will always remain, as do the memories. They wait patiently for us to join them in the afterlife and tell us there is no death, only eternal life. Angels encourage us to communicate with loved ones in the afterlife if we desire it, and if our loved one is available and in agreement. When you send prayers to a loved one, the process is the same as communicating with angels. Ask your angel if your loved ones are able to communicate with you. If they are, communicate by thought or speak out loud your message. As mentioned before, you may receive their message in thought, hear an inner voice, receive it as a mental vision, or in the dream state.

During periods of contemplation and dreaming, I have received personal messages from several family members in the afterlife. In some cases, I have expanded my awareness to their location and visually encountered them on a higher plane. This has given me peace of mind and a better understanding of life in higher realms. My dreams of these higher planes and communication with those present are as clear and reassuring as those in my wakeful reality. Sri Harold Klemp reminds us that dreams are real experiences from another time, place, or dimension. Of course, it is important to record all communication and dreams from angels, spirit guides, and deceased family and friends. All messages and visions will give you some insight into the heavenly planes and activities on those planes. The following example is a clairaudience message I received six months after the death of my sister.

Message from A Loved One

* We (deceased family members) are with you now, and have been since we left Earth.
* We are watching over you, protecting you, and keeping you safe.
* We join you in your dreams, but you may not remember them when you awake.
* We are closer to you than you think—expect to feel our presence.
* We receive your loving thoughts and blessings and send our love to you.
* We are working with angels here and have grown greatly with their guidance.

* Our absence is only an illusion, for we are with you in
  spirit.
* One day people on Earth will understand that those
  who died are fully alive and well in new bodies and
  residing on higher planes.

When we think of a deceased loved one, we are actually sending telepathic thoughts to them. Take the next step, and speak to them during periods of contemplation and prayer. You may receive an inner vision, spoken words, intuitive impression, or experience a feeling of closeness. For example, I received a comforting message from my sister several months after her death. She describing the profound beauty of the place she was in. She repeated often that there is no death, only life more beautiful than ever. She also describes her translation experience, detaching from her body with ease, and seeing herself above her body and looking down as she lay in the hospital bed. She was aware of and heard all that transpired, feeling no pain or fear, only a disengaged curiosity. She reported seeing the white light and feeling a powerful, loving and beautiful force surrounding her and drawing her toward the light with great speed. Next, she found herself free, in a lighter body, greeted by family and friends in a beautiful and serene place beyond description. On several occasions, while in the dream state, I found myself in her presence as we visited and soul traveled together.

We all have the ability to communicate with God, Lord Christ, The Holy Spirit, angels, ascended masters, spirit guides, and loved ones in higher planes. The information from higher sources is available to all seekers of the light. Your deceased loved ones may also be serving as our spirit guides and protectors. It is now commonly accepted and shared, that messages from deceased loved ones can come to us in a variety of ways – dreams, visions, a soft touch, through the movement of objects, symbols, footsteps, and other sounds and sights. Therefore, be attentive and do not doubt your capacity to receive messages and communicate with those in the celestial realms.

Reincarnation - Returned Trip

I would be remiss if I did not include the subject of reincarnation—our return trip to Earth. Many people in our society have accepted the belief that we continue to reincarnate to Earth until this earthly experience is no longer required for the soul's progression. Such beliefs have been part of eastern religions and philosophies for ages. Reincarnation can be defined as rebirth – the coming and going of Soul into a new body each time It enters the lower planes. Our society now considers reincarnation not only a strong possibility, but also in some cases, a scientific fact, based on research and documented interviews of individuals who recall their past lives. There are many misconceptions around the doctrine of reincarnation. Dr. Spencer Lewis is but one of many authors who have expressed their views on this subject. His explanation is that:

"The personality is distinct and unique with each being. This personality manifests in the human body during its earthly life as the ego or character of the person, and at transition moves on and into the Cosmic Plane along with the Soul Essence. It will remain on the higher plane until the right time comes for another incarnation of the Soul Essence in another physical body for additional earthly experiences. This also will be added to the Personality memory, and remain intact there as the accumulating knowledge and wisdom of the inner self. The Personality remains conscious of itself on the Cosmic Plane, as it is conscious of itself on the Earth plane. Each personality may incarnate many times - the limit is unknown. It never retrogrades or enters the bodies of lower animals" (Rosicrucian Manual, 189).

My study and practice as a hypnotherapist suggests that we have returned many, many times to Earth in cycles of death and birth. In some lives, we were males and in other lives, females. We were poor, rich, rulers, and servants. In some lifetimes, we lived to old age. At other times, our lives are cut short. Each of our lifetimes is but a day in a continuous cycle of lifetimes. However, it may be hundreds of years (in Earth time) before our next rebirth on Earth, in which case we will be returning to a very different world than the one we left. There are new challenges and opportunities for growth in each returning lifetime. What we accomplished in past lifetimes will determine our destiny on our return trips. We often return with the same soul group, those who reincarnate about the same time and have emotional ties with us from previous lifetimes. We often pick up where we left off in our former lives on Earth; there may be a reversal of roles, such as being a mother in one lifetime and then your daughter becomes your mother in another lifetime. This enables us to have a variety of roles and experiences over many lifetimes.

Newhouse and Isaac (1998) inform us that the Kindel Archangel works with all souls long before they incarnate on Earth again. He is present when we view our past life graphs so we can see how our next life might best be spent. The Archangel helps us choose our gender, parents, birth country, life work, and so much more, in the coming lifetime to ensure that we cancel karmic debt and utilize our acquired abilities and talents. This Archangel also painstakingly forms our Incarnation Disc, our spiritual DNA, and places it in the heart region of our mental body. He appears to use again after death during a careful review of our earthly performance, including how we handled lessons, challenges, relationships and opportunities (Isaac, Stephen & Phyllis, 2006).

With each earthly lifetime, we experience either the positive benefits or natural consequences of our past lives, known as the Law of Karma. Archangel Michael and his warrior Angels belong to the celestial hierarchy called Powers, who guide the Laws of Cause and Effect. They operate on the etheric plane just above the mental plane. These legions of light are always present in any major catastrophe, where they do all they can, within karmic restrictions, to help us avoid disaster and defend us against the dark forces. Nevertheless, we are reminded that our goal in this incarnation is to learn to live on this lower material plane, while keeping our spiritual connection with our true heavenly home. Furthermore, our highest purpose in this incarnation is to dwell in the Divine Light of the Holy Spirit, so that it will serve as our guide in this life and our future lives on higher planes.

The history of previous lives on Earth and in the Spirit world is stored in our subconscious. Glimpses of our earthly past lives may appear in our dreams. We have the capacity to recall a past life when regressed back to a former lifetime, by a competent past-life therapist or hypnotherapist. Some people have experienced flashbacks of former lives during their travels, or had a feeling of knowing a person or place from a previous lifetime.

For example, Jenny Cockell, one of many authors with books about memories and visions of past lives, described in *Across Time and Death* (1993), her life as Mary Sulton, an Irish woman who died during childbirth in the 1930s. Cockell's book details past memories of that lifetime, and her search for records about Mary's life and those of her living children. With the aid of a past life regression therapist, she recalled in detail her life during that time period. With much searching, Cockell was able to reconnect with her (Mary's) children, who accepted the convincing proof that she was indeed their deceased mother who died in the early 1930s. In Cockell's latest book, *Past Lives, Future Lives* 1996, she describes additional past lives and details of events and locations of these lives, again with follow-up verification of birth records at these locations. Cockell has the unusual ability to not only recall her past lives, but also visualize several future lives where she later returns to Earth, as a female in a very changed world of the twenty-third century.

We have an untapped capacity to recall past life events and also see into the future. We can train our minds to expand and project across dimensions in time and space. Regression (past life/event viewing), and progression (future life/remote viewing), occurs more frequently than most people are willing to accept. Certainly, if people can be trained or have the ability to see events/things occurring in distant locations, or see across time and space to potential events in the future, then perhaps we can be trained to remember our past lives and view our potential future.

Cayce, known as the "sleeping prophet," gave fourteen thousand life readings over a forty-three year period. Approximately 2,000 readings dealt with the subject of reincarnation. These readings were given to help individuals understand their soul strengths and weaknesses, as well as their talents and potential in this life. The Association of Research and Enlightenment (ARE) has a wealth of books and online information on the topic of reincarnation. Other excellent sources of information are Dr. Winafred Blake Lucas' books on past-life therapy, in particular *Regression Therapy: A Handbook for Professionals,* which contains documented case histories of reincarnation events. Regression therapists use age regression, a process of moving a client backward in time chronologically. This approach is used to obtain early childhood and even prior lifetime memories, especially those issues and patterns that are affecting one's current mental and physical health. When we ascend to higher levels of consciousness, past life memories will be recalled with new awareness and we will be able to understand mistakes of the past and, hopefully, not repeat them in future lifetimes.

The following chapter examines the question, as benefactors of Mother Earth, what can we do to promote a more heavenly and peaceful planet?

6

CREATE A HEAVEN
ON EARTH

All Things are Possible

Humanity is well on its way in embracing the path to enlightenment. We have broken away from the old doomsday prophecies and have taken back our power, for human momentum is too great to hold us back. Earth is the planet of free choice; we can change what we don't like for something better. We either accept responsibility for our actions, or deny our responsibilities. There is no pre-destination, only the agreement to experience what you have chosen to manifest. This year and beyond humanity has the potential to shift to a higher conscious awakening. Do you choose to remain in the old consciousness and thinking patterns, or will you join with others to take the great leap forward in global ascension of the human race.

Is it possible to create a Heaven on Earth? For many, the answer is "maybe, it is possible." The evolution of human consciousness is proceeding in this direction, aided by Earth's higher love vibrations, for the purpose of expanding human awareness of its divine missions. The forces of darkness in our midst are slowly but surely being defeated, righting the wrongs that have long been perpetrated on humankind. Humanity suffers when natural laws are misused for selfish purpose or materialistic greed. We cannot be responsible for the mistakes (sins) of others, only our own. Good intentions and deeds will evidently overcome the sins of the world, for divine law is a powerful balancer in life.

We are experiencing a period of transition in which the heavenly hosts of angels, ascended masters, great spiritual teachers, and Divine Spirit are directing their powerful energies toward the enlightenment and transformation of the planet. The destiny of the planet is to become a heavenly place of love, joy, and peace. Step by step, we are marching toward this goal. You ask, what will this look like? Angels have informed me that this new reality will be interdimensional in nature. Humans will expand their five senses, and extrasensory perceptions. This will include an awareness of inner worlds and invisible dimensions of life. Many are already using their intuitive ability to perceive, and experience the unseen presence of nature spirit beings, and other life forms. For some, the ability to receive telepathic thoughts from other people and heavenly sources, to channel higher beings, and to hear inner voices and heavenly music (clairaudience) has already become their reality. Many more people today are experiencing a sense of clear knowing, inner visions, revelations, and intuition to guide them in life. Using our higher perceptive skills will allow us to travel consciously to other planes and locations while our physical body remains at rest at home. As Humanity ascends, Earth will be become more like the mid-astral plane where many souls reside after death.

Perhaps you have noticed the growing number of local networking groups quietly promoting world peace, humanitarian and ecological causes, natural and holistic health care, honest governments, and integrity in business affairs. People in all walks of life throughout the world are focusing on peaceful and nonviolent solutions to world problems, and for health, happiness and prosperity for all. What is occurring has not made headline news, but it does make news on internets around the world that globally connect, and inform people on ways to make positive life changes.

Some skeptics believe world peace will never happen because of the number of warlike and hostile societies on the planet. Certainly, those who focus their attention on materialism and greed will be blind to any form of a peaceful planet. However, I, along with many others on the planet, hold a vision that the peoples of the world will overcome the dark forces facing us today. Anxiety, stress, confusion, and fearfulness have produced outward strife and discontent in the world. Until we realize inner peace, there will be no outward manifestation of peace on the planet. We are seeing people of all ages, nationalities, and creeds coming together to create a more prosperous and joy-filled life. They are taking the steps in fulfilling the promise made by Archangel Michael to the peoples of Earth, "that the old chaotic Earth will fall into oblivion and a new Earth, or state of consciousness, will rise out of it".

Spiritually Centering -The Next Steps

We are now witnessing the cleansing, purification, and conquering of lower thought patterns on Earth. Let us all embrace the light and follow its path to hasten the day of peace and harmony. During this time of change, consider these spiritually centering steps:

1. Remain God-centered, focusing on what is good, positive, and beneficial in the world, instead of what is wrong with people and situations in your life.
2. Commit to the transformation of the earth by using your talents and skills to work for world peace and to improve the quality of life locally, nationally and globally for the world's population.
3. Accept all people on Earth as members of one united family and extend your love and compassion to all regions of the planet.
4. Be a supportive presence for those who have lost loved ones in death and compassionately support those facing life transitions.
5. Be detached from the confusion, turmoil, hostility and corruption around you and maintain inner peace during times of chaos. When you align your mind with Divine Mind, you will have confidence in your ability to handle all challenges.

6. Be patient and welcome the opportunities to expand your thinking by seeking out enlightened individuals who can help you evolve to a higher level of consciousness, create positive changes, and support a new reality for the planet.

7. Take responsibility for your words and actions by not blaming others for your misfortunes and mistakes, and practice nonjudgmental acceptance of other people's cultural and religious beliefs.

8. Visualize living on a peaceful planet where everyone feels safe, prosperous, and enjoys liberty, freedom, and self-realization. Plan your life as if this new reality is already here.

9. Remember that heaven is within each person's state of mind and we have the power to create, empower and transform the world.

10. Become a beacon of light for others to follow by illuminating, inspiring, and empowering others to express their highest purpose in life.

Beacons of Light

Beacons of light are people who connect other people to their inner light source and the higher frequencies of love, harmony and peace. Help people to combine with the higher universal light frequencies of unconditional love, harmony, and peace in healing humanity and the planet. Let your indwelling spirit radiate unconditional love for all life forms. Form networks of light workers to show others how to awaken their heart centers and connect with their inner light, the divine spirit within. Demonstrate how they can breathe in the universe's revitalizing energy force and breathe out fear, distress, negative emotions, and release toxins from their body and mind. Help others to use their indwelling God for guidance, making right decisions and taking perfect actions. Moreover, be confident, fearless, and undaunted in spreading your lights throughout the world. Yes, you can do this and more, as points of loving lights, pointing the way in illuminating the world with thoughts of inner peace, love and harmony.

By our deeds, we can make a difference in the lives of others. Collectively, we can accomplish much when working in small groups. Such groups, unified in their intentions, can spread across the globe to become a critical mass of consciously aware people who are beacons of illumination, showing the way for others to navigate safely. We have witnessed, throughout time that united, and dedicated groups of people, however small their numbers, can change the course of history.

Empowerment and humanitarian groups around the world are raising the consciousness of humanity and envisioning a better world. Use your talents and skills to usher in the new paradigm for global peace on the planet. Encourage people to participate in events that will spread more light and compassion in the world. I also encourage you to write a personal declaration statement as to ways you can serve as a light worker, and help others use their inner lights for peaceful and loving purposes.

My Personal Declaration

For example, I have included a simple declaration statement for you, and other light workers with similar intentions. My declaration consists of the following truths for me:

I acknowledge that spiritual truths serve to guide my daily life and my thoughts create the reality I experience in life. My reality is focused on soul/God realization, and the divine mission for humankind. I surrender my heart and mind to this Divine Source of light, love, and harmony, and allow it to flow through me into the world. As a light worker, I will hold in consciousness an image of a harmonious, peaceful, and a prosperous world. May this vision be manifested in the world, and in the hearts and minds of all those who are working towards a higher conscious awakening on planet Earth.

Prepare now, for the day of awakening is at hand. Center your thoughts and intentions by aligning them with your indwelling Spirit. Release all fears about tomorrow and maintain a peaceful center where the stillness of God resides. Accept God's divine plan for the planet and rejoice that you have been chosen to participate in its manifestation. This is not the time to lose faith in humankind, for all will have a role in the planetary awakening. Do your part and follow your inner guidance when making decisions and taking action. Eckhart Tolle's book, *A New Earth - Awakening To Your Life's Purpose* (2005), informs us that the evolution of humanity will bring a shift from horizontal awareness to vertical awareness, and that we must remain in the now moment by aligning ourselves with the universal purpose for humanity. In so doing, we will experience acceptance, enjoyment, and enthusiasm in what we do.

It is also important to disregard the negativity in the world and those who will try to discredit efforts for peace. Leave behind all things that no longer serve your highest good and pursue the goals for the creation of a more heavenly world. Develop an inner connection with Divine Spirit and choose the spiritual path that will lead you eventually to your heavenly home. When the call for service comes, joyfully step forward and take your place with others in ushering in a new heavenly world.

7

SET YOUR INTENTIONS

Great Expectations

We are told the Old World, as you know it, is coming to an end. A New World is even now being formed and will become more visible soon. The New World will be a place of peace and love, a place that shares reality with higher dimensions in the universe, and a place where human consciousness is expressed in higher frequencies of light and sound. Before this new reality is manifested expect to experience more discontent, anxiety, and confusion as the world evolves to higher levels of consciousness. This is the time that humanity has longed for, and the time to perform our roles in manifesting the new world. Choose now your intentions and begin the process of letting go of all that holds you to the past. Prepare yourselves to experience all that is coming with an open mind. Place your attention first on the small changes in your beliefs, emotional expressions and detachment from past burdens. Expand your awareness, sharper your perceptions, and focus your thoughts on a peaceful and life-giving planet.

Slowly, the old world will dissolve along with the darkness on the planet. The new dawn on the planet will come as a surprise to the unaware, but not for those enlightened souls who have worked hard to bring forth a brighter and more unified world. This will be a true awakening, long sought throughout the ages, and seen as starting point for a new age of enlightenment. Earth will change in many ways and places to support an enlightened society. Humans and all species will evolve together and begin to communicate by thought transmission. All life will respond to positive, loving, and compassionate thoughtful actions, and will thrive immediately. Each person will know his or her mission, and will joyfully participate with others in assuring a peaceful, healthy, and bountiful planet. Your mission is to share this good news with others and prepare to fulfill earth's destiny.

Therefore, accept with great anticipation our changing world. There is no turning back to the old days and ways, for they are passing quickly away. A new day in world history is unfolding for all to experience. Human consciousness is expanding quickly to receive the higher frequencies on the planet. More people will feel hopeful, optimistic, and unified in their efforts to make positive changes. This optimistic energy will spread across the planet, from the smallest villages to the greatest cities, as humanity embrace new opportunities for advancement. However, each person must accept responsibility for making positive changes in their local and state areas. The wave of moving forward, planning for a more peaceful and abundant world will need thoughtful planning and serious group action. Those who have the most will be encouraged to freely share their resources with those with many needs, for the equalization of wealth sharing is necessary for a prosperous world. Even now, many are finding they can live with less and still enjoy an abundant life. This expanded awareness is already in the human collective consciousness, and will evidently become the new reality on the planet.

Begin now to release, let go, and give away what is not wanted or needed in your life. Modify your living standards, travel light on your path and appreciate the abundance that is yours now. For many have lost much from fires, floods, severe storms and other disasters, but find they can adapt and still survive on less and have inner peace and happiness. A simpler lifestyle, without the clutter of more material things and gadgets is very freeing for the soul. This enables us to enjoy abundance, natural resources and beauty that our planet offers, and helps us to appreciate its spiritual nature.

What is My Role?

You asked, what is my role during this time of planetary changes? It is to be at peace with all the changes that are occurring on the planet at this time. It is to lift your thoughts to the highest levels by accepting the will of Divine Spirit with grace, gratitude and love. It is to become detached from old destructive thought patterns, and accept the divine aspects of your multidimensional soul/selves. You can do this by turning within to the All-

Knowing Source of Wisdom for answers and guidance. You can expand your inner vision to include a world filled with love and harmony that embraces all life forms. You can manifest, through your good deeds, a new world where all will thrive, lives peacefully, and protect Mother Earth's resources. Continue to hold in your consciousness the highest vibratory frequencies of loving light, and use it to manifest a more heavenly world.

Celestial beings send their greetings and are celebrating the shift in our taking responsible action for a better world. The energy around the planet is very strong and forceful, and will move humankind in the direction of advancement and peace. Expect more waves of energy that will eventually lead to positive changes in our governmental, economic, social, health and educational systems. All of us, including animals, will feel some anxiety and discomfort with this increase energy wave. There will also be societal confusion, and stress, as the old systems are slowly dismantled and replaced with more functional systems. Those who cannot accept the changes on the planet will leave it and return at a future time. Those who remain will experience major challenges, and must prepare now to adapt to a period of global climate change, and economic and societal instability. These uncertainties will create fear and unrest in some localities, and there will be the need to find solutions quickly before chaotic situations take hold. World leaders must remain calm and show compassion when implementing sound solutions. The solutions must focus on unifying diverse population groups to work responsibly for positive outcomes. World leaders must be held accountable for their decisions and actions.

Now is the time for each person to contemplate their vision of a new world and its relationship with the universe. The present time is eternity, forever presenting itself for viewing and experiencing. Consider the ebb and flow of life around you, embracing all with love, and be attentive to the voice/sound and vision/light of God sending forth messages for your Soul's growth. And finally, contemplate on the issues facing our world today and what proposals you would offer for the healing of the planet.

Closing Remarks

My vision for the future is that humanity will show more compassion and exhibit a strong desire to heal the planet and protect her vital resources, while initiating new social-economic and educational delivery systems. My hope is that people around the world will gather in small study and discussion groups, and use social networks, such as Facebook, Twitter, and other social medium networks to share ideas, discuss social changes, and plan for the future. Optimism, co-operation, purposefulness, harmony, and unity will become living symbols for the planet, as the human races move forward to embrace and celebrate its evolutionary advancement. I believe that the divine plan for Earth has been written in the great wisdom books of old, and well go forward and manifest in this planetary cycle. With regret, I realize that those of my generation will have translated, and will not be present to see the rebirth of a revitalize planet. It will be up to younger generations to carry the torchlight to victory.

I am aware that some readers may be skeptical about the information in this book and will want to explore and investigate on their own. If the subject of angels, higher planes, and Earth changes are new to you, I invite you to explore these topics further. My reading references are a good beginning, but also consider discussion groups on the topics in this book and other books on the evolutionary process occurring on the planet and in human consciousness. Also include topics on the principles of earth's cycles of human transitions and advancement.

Many are aware of the strong winds of change blowing over the face of the planet and urging us to align ourselves with the evolutional changes now occurring. Now is the time for us to collaborate with others and become positive forces in the global wave for peace and enlightenment on the planet. I join you in your efforts and look forward to the day we all can celebrate the arrival of a higher conscious awakening for humankind.

Reciting affirmations for inner peace and a positive attitude during challenging times can be extremely helpful. You can use the ones below or write your own to focus your thoughts.

Affirmations

On Listening: I listen to the still small voice within me. I give my full attention to the Infinite Presence that guides me to experience greater peace and joy. I listen for the inner voice of divine spirit to guide and protect me in my daily activities.

On Change: I welcome change in my life. As my thoughts and beliefs evolve to include more of my spiritual nature, my world changes to reflect the new degrees of my awareness. I know change is good because it helps me grow spiritually.

On Releasing Tension: I know that my deep connection with Divine Spirit enables me to know that everything is in perfect order, and working for my highest good. Realizing this truth, all my tension is release. I am relaxed, at ease, and living in perfect peace.

On Spiritual Inspiration: I accept the divine light and love energy that is always available to me, and open my heart to receive the loving blessings from Divine Spirit. I am spiritually inspired to become a beacon of light to promote a higher conscious awakening on planet, and serve as an inspiration for other to follow my example.

On Trusting: I trust in the wisdom and guidance of Divine Mind expressing in my life as universe love, peace, harmony, and order. I attract people, situations, and ideas that best bring the spiritual perfection of life into my experience. I trust in God to guide me through every experience as I learn, spiritual grow, and fulfill my earthly mission.

May the blessings of Divine Spirit guide your life's journey and may you be a channel for peace, Divine Love and unity in the world.

8

EXPAND YOUR AWARENESS WITH HU LOVE SONG

The HU Song Exercise

Sri Harold Klemp, spiritual leader of Eckankar- Religion of the Light and Sound of God has thousands of followers throughout the world who sing HU, an ancient name for God, as a daily practice. Sing HU (pronounced like the word "hue") is a song that can expand your awareness, bring comfort, inner peace and guidance, protection, healing,and fill you with divine love and light, and much more for your total well-being and state of higher conscious awakening. Join me and thousands of other people around the world who are singing the HU song in small and large groups or along as a daily spiritual exercise.

More information about the HU Song can
be found at (www.Eckankar.org)

References

Association for Research and Enlightenment Inc. (1992). *Mind–The Edgar Cayce Readings, Volume 20.* Virginia Beach, VA. A.R.E. Press.

Bailey, Alice. (1980). *Esoteric Healing,* N.Y.: Lucis Publishing Company.

Branden, Gregg. (1997). *Awakening To Zero Point: The Collective Initiation,* Bellevue, WA: Radio Bookstore Press.

Carey, Ken. (1986). *Vision.* Kansas City, Missouri: c/o UNI*SUN.

_____(Raphael). (1986). The *Starseed Transmissions.* Kansas City, Missouri: UNI*SUN.

Carroll, Lee. (1993). *Kryon: The End Times,* Del Mar, CA: The Kryon Writings, Inc.

_____(1997). *Kryon: Partnering with God,* Del Mar, CA: The Kryon Writings, Inc.

_____(1997). *Kryon 2000: Passing the Marker,* Book 8. Del Mar, CA: The Kryon Writings, Inc.

Cayce, Hugh Lynn & Edgar Cayce. (1998). No *Death-God's Other Door*. Virginia Beach, VA: A.R.E. Press.

Chaney, Earlyne. (1988). *The Mystery of Death and Dying*. York Beach, Maine: Samuel Weiser, Inc.

Cockell, Jenny. (1996). *Past Lives, Future Lives*. New York, N.Y: A Fireside Book/Simon & Schuster Press.

Colton, Ann Ree. (1973).*Watch Your Dreams*. Glendale, CA: ABC Publishing Company.

Daniel, Alma, Timothy Wyllie, and Andrew Ramer. (1992). *Ask Your Angels*. N.Y.: Ballantine Books.

Dubro, Peggy Phoenix, and David Lapierre. (2002). *Elegant Empowerment: Evolution of Consciousness*. Norwich, CT.: Platinum Publishing House.

Fox, Emmet. (1967). *Reincarnation*. Marina del Ray, CA: DeVorss & Company.

Grant, Robert. (1994). *Are We Listening to the Angels?* Virginia Beach, Va.: A.R.E. Press.

_____(2003). Universe of Worlds: Exploring the Frontiers of the Afterlife. Virginia Beach, Va.: A.R.E. Press.

Heindel, Max. (1984). *Occult Principles of Health and Healing*. Oceanside, CA: The Rosicrucian Fellowship Press.

Holmes, Ernest. (1998). *The Science of Mind*. NY: Penguin Putnam Inc.

_____(1999). *Can We Talk To God?* Deerfield, Fl: Health Communications, Inc.

_____(2002). *The Essentials –Ernest Holmes*. NY: Penguin Putnam Inc.

Klemp, Harold. (2003). *Eckankar-Ancient Wisdom for Today*. Minneapolis, MN: Eckankar Publication.

_____(1999). *The Art of Spiritual Dreaming.* Minneapolis, MN: Eckankar Publication.

_____(1992). *The Easy Way Discourses.* Minneapolis, MN: Eckankar Publication.

Isaac, Stephen and Phyllis. (2006). *The Collected Works of Flower A. Newhouse.* San Diego, CA: The Christward Ministry.

Kubis, Pat, and Macy, Mark. (1995). *Conversations Beyond the Light.* Boulder, CO: Griffin Publishing.

Lewis, Spencer. (1963). *Rosicrucian Manual.* San Jose, CA: AMORC Press.

Locher, Theo, and Maggy Harsch-Fischbach. (1963). *Breakthroughs in Technical Spirit Communication.* Boulder, CO: Continuing Life Research.

Lucas, Winafred Blake. (1993). *Regression Therapy: A Handbook for Professionals.* Crest Park, CA: Deep Forest Press.

Mark, Barbara, and Trudy Griswold. (1995). *Angelspeak*: *How to Talk with Your Angels.* NY: Simon and Schuster.

Maynard, Marianne. (2009). *Take Charge of Your Thoughts – Create Your Ideal Life.* New York, N.Y., Strategic Book Publishing.

Newhouse, Flower & Isaac, Stephen. (1998). *Touched by Angels.* Woodside, CA: Bluster Communications.

O'Neil, Kim. (1995). *How to Talk with Your Angels.* NY: Avon Books

Roberts, Jane. (1972). *Seth Speaks.* NY: Bantam Books.

Sechrist, Elsie. (1992). *Death Does Not Part Us.* Virginia Beach, Va.: A.R.E. Press.

Smith, Robert. (1993). *In The Presence of Angels.* Virginia Beech: A.R.E. Press.

Study Group #1 of Association for Research and Enlightenment, Inc. (1970). *A Search for God. Books 1 and 11*. Reprint, Virginia Beach, Va.: A.R.E. Press.

Tolle, Eckhart. (2005). *A New Earth: Awakening to Your Life's Purpose*. NY: Dutton/Penguin Group.

Twitchell, Paul. (1978). *Letters to Gail*. Menlo Park, CA: Illumintaled Way Press.

Virtue, Doreen. (1997). *Angel Therapy*. Carlsbad, CA.: Hay House, Inc.

_____(1999). *Healing with Angels*. Carlsbad, CA.: Hay House, Inc.

Yin, Omorah Quan. (1996) *Pleiadian Perspectives on Human Evolution*. Santa Fe, NM: Bear and Company.

PERSONAL NOTE SHEET

THE AUTHOR

Dr. Maynard has a BA and M.Ed. in art education, a post-degree in occupational therapy, and a Ph.D. in Behavioral Sciences, with emphasis on Rehabilitation Psychology and Gerontology. She has published over fifty articles in professional journals and has authored several books. As a former professor of health sciences, her career pursuits included occupational therapy, mental health, gerontology, and continuing education/staff development. Dr. Maynard is a National Board Certified Counselor and Gerontological Counselor, and has received honorary recognition for her professional teaching, research and community service, in mental health, occupational therapy, and gerontology education, besides international consultation. Her current interests include spirituality in the mature years, life transitions, holistic health practice, and her own journey to higher consciousness awakening.